Everyday Words and Creative Practice:
Ten Australian Poets in Conversation

Everyday Words and Creative Practice: Ten Australian Poets in Conversation

Edited by Jen Webb and Monica Carroll

With interviews conducted by
Jen Webb and Kevin Brophy

PUNCHER & WATTMANN

First published in 2019
Published by Puncher and Wattmann
PO Box 279
Waratah NSW 2298

http://www.puncherandwattmann.com
puncherandwattmann@bigpond.com

ISBN: 9781925780178

A catalogue record for this book is available from the National Library Australia.

Cover design by Miranda Douglas
Text design by Christine Bruderlin
Printed by Lightning Source International

This project has been assisted by the Australian Government through the Australia Council, its arts funding and advisory body.

Contents

Dedication

To Dr Sandra Burr, researcher; writer; poet; and animal ethicist, whose departure has left a hole we have never been able to fill.

Acknowledgments

We acknowledge the hard-working Research Office team at the University of Canberra, who helped with the funding application, and Dr Karen Mow, research developer *par excellence*, who generously provided us with feedback, critical direction and insights that helped ensure that our proposal was fundable. We gratefully acknowledge the Australian Research Council for providing the money that paid for our travel to meet and interview poets around the world; the poets who gave so generously of their time and thoughts; the transcribers who turned our often-shonky recordings into coherent transcripts; and the contributions of the late Dr Sandra Burr, who organised and administered the project.

We acknowledge the support of the Australian Research Council, 'Understanding creative excellence: A case study in poetry' (DP130100402).

Chief Investigator's Introduction

In the late 2000s three people—all of us both poets and university-based scholars—began talking seriously about starting an investigation into the links between poetry, knowledge and creativity. For well over a decade we had observed, and been intimately involved in, the growing number of creative writers enrolling in doctoral degrees and, rather than following the conventional path of literary analysis, using the processes and movements of their own creative writing to build knowledge about the topic, question or problem that interested them. This may seem *de rigueur* now, after more than twenty years of creative doctorates being conducted and completed by artists at universities across Australia, but ten or fifteen years ago it took some argument to explain and justify what was going on in that domain, and why taxpayer-funded doctorates could legitimately be pursued in creative mode.

For at least as long, all three of us had also been writing poetry; reading poetry; exploring the scholarly and technical literature on poetry; reading what poets said about their own work and its motivating factors; and thinking about how poetry makes—if not the world, at least fractions of that world—go round. And we had researched and published extensively on related issues: Kevin Brophy focusing on creativity, Paul Magee on knowledge, and Jen Webb on creative research. Building on this background and on our shared interests, we completed a pilot project on the question of poetry and knowledge, and then began the slow process of applying for funding. At this point the University of Hertfordshire's Professor Michael Biggs—a leading international figure in the field of arts research—joined the team. Together we structured a project titled 'Understanding Creative Excellence: a case study in poetry', and gratefully accepted funding from the Australian Research Council.

We chose to focus on poetry not only because three of the researchers are poets but also, and more specifically, because poetry is (pretty much) *sui generis* in the broader literary field.[1] Other genres and modes of writing are, by and large, committed to communication, whether of ideas, story or information. Poetry, by contrast, is not focused on communication, largely because it deals with the ineffable, with that which resists or escapes codification. Hence poetry engages more consistently with the sensory and with imagery than with communicative clarity; hence, as Auden famously wrote, 'poetry makes nothing happen'.[2]

Moreover, of all literary modes poetry is perhaps the one least committed to instrumentality: it has a very minor presence in the Australian curriculum, and there is neither a popular audience nor large-scale market-oriented production for contemporary English-language poetry. The various reports produced by cultural economist David Throsby bear this out. His 2015 reports show that poetry has virtually no footprint in the larger publisher category, but relies on small and micro-publishers and therefore experiences a more limited distribution network than do children's books, literary and genre fiction, and creative nonfiction.[3] Not surprisingly, poets receive the lowest income of all Australian writers, by a substantial margin. As Throsby's team reports, the average gross income from writing in the 2013/2014 financial year reached only $4,000 for poets, compared with $12,900 for all writers.[4]

Despite this apparent condition of deficit in the art form, there is a substantial population of poets across the world, possessed of substantial social, intellectual and cultural capital. On the whole poets are highly educated, reflective and engaged individuals whose poetry, prose, and knowledge transfer practices add considerable value to their communities. Despite their comparative exclusion from the world of money and social recognition, they keep producing poetry, keep connecting with other poets, writers and scholars, and show considerable skill in innovation and in community building.

We chose poetry as the site for our investigation into creativity for these reasons, and because that exclusion reduces the variables. In the first instance, poetry is produced for its own sake, and for the satisfaction of the poet. Another driver might be the acquisition of social and cultural capital but (to use Bourdieu's phrase) poetry's 'emancipation . . . from the rule of money and interest'[5] means that the investments of time, education, and effort are motivated primarily by the drive to create. By contrast, other fields of creative endeavour, particularly business and science, are necessarily motivated as much by the need to generate a financial or knowledge return. Poetry's 'freedom' may result in a small social, political and economic footprint, but this 'freedom' allows it to act as a site of rich experimentation, cross-art collaboration, art for art's sake practice and creative play.

In his Interviewer's Introduction (below) Kevin Brophy explains something of the recruitment process in which we engaged; this resulted in interviews with seventy-six poets, of whom twenty-one are Australian. Kevin notes in his introduction that though each of the poets answered the same suite of questions, their responses, what they chose to emphasise, and perhaps above all their voices, are highly individual. For the researchers, as we moved from interview to analysis, this was compelling material, and we have published extensively elsewhere on our findings.

Something we did not expect to find, but which became evident from this research, is that collaboration—or at least robust connection with others—is an important aspect of creativity, whether in an art form or in other fields of endeavour. There have been many publications over the past decade that strongly argue against the myth of isolation, and note that collaboration is at the heart of 'excellent'—that is to say, influential, widely recognised—practice.[6]

Though the logic of collaboration is not complex in and of itself, actually performing collaboration is extraordinarily complex. No theories can fully explain what might go on in any relationship; no amount of experience prepares an individual for any new project; and no matter how long you have been researching and / or writing with someone else, with each new project you start again from the beginning. Despite such widely recognised complexities, collaboration is a highly desirable value and practice, not least because—the literature suggests—it leads to efficient and effective achievement of outcomes.[7] However, that literature is generally premised on the (unexpressed) notion of a 'perfect partnership', where complementary skills and shared aspirations lead to quality work and a satisfying experience.

This doesn't often happen, principally because the Perfect Partnership is akin to Plato's ideal Form: it doesn't appear in the lived world, because people are neither eternal nor immutable; they are not abstractions, but messy and flawed creatures filled with tangential thoughts, idiosyncratic memories and bad habits. This does not condemn us to suffer the inverse of Plato's Form—the temporary, the fickle and the flawed. Rather, it can remind us that to collaborate effectively in creative practice requires ethical engagement, patience, and enthusiasm. It can also remind artists that collaboration is a great way to shake up their own practice. As the poet Geraldine Monk points out, we can really only escape the straitjacket of our 'entrenchments'— habitual ways of making and thinking—if we are 'truly disrupted by the invasive undermining or enhancement of an other. This other is "collaboration"'.[8] What we learned, in the course of this three-year, nine-nation, four-researcher, seventy-six-poet project is that the poets seek out ways to escape that straitjacket; and find themselves enlivened by, entwined with, others. However loose the weave may be, each poet finds in other people and their writings, ways to examine and extend their own practice, and ways to keep going.

Jen Webb

NOTES

1   Webb, J. 2018 'Poetry and the conditions of practice: A field study', in
     James Albright, Deborah Hartman and Jacqueline Widin, eds, *Bourdieu's
     Field Theory and the Social Sciences* (pp. 53–66), Basingstoke: Palgrave
     Macmillan

2   Auden, W. H. 2007 'In memory of WB Yeats', in E. Mendelson, ed,
     Collected Poems (p. 247), New York: Modern Library. Originally published
     in 1940

3   Throsby, D., Zwar, J., and Morgan, C. 2018 *Australian Book Publishers in
     the Global Industry: Survey Method and Results*, Research paper 1 (February),
     Sydney: Macquarie University

4   Zwar, J., Throsby, D. and Longden, T. 2015 *Australian Authors Industry Brief
     No. 3: Authors' Income. The Australian Book Industry: Authors, Publishers and
     Readers in a Time of Change*, Sydney: Macquarie University

5   Bourdieu, P. 2010 *Sociology is a Martial Art: Political Writings*, translated by
     P. P. Ferguson, R. Nice and L. Wacquant, New York: New Press, p. 222

6   See, for example: Pheby, A. 2010 'The myth of isolation: Its effect on literary
     culture and creative writing as a discipline', *Creative Writing: Teaching
     Theory & Practice* 2.1: 51–58; John-Steiner, V. 2000 *Creative Collaboration*,
     Oxford: Oxford University Press; Webb, J. and Melrose, A. 2015 'Writers
     Inc: Writing and collaborative practice', in A. Peary and T. Hunley, eds,
     Creative Writing Pedagogies for the Twenty-First Century (pp. 102–25),
     Carbondale: Southern Illinois University Press; Webb, J. and Hetherington,
     P. 2016 'Slipperiness, strange attractors, and collaborative sociability', *Axon:
     Creative Explorations* 6.1; Webb, J. and Carroll, M. 2017 'A seethe of poets:
     Creativity and community', *TEXT* Special Issue 40

7   See, e.g., Sohal, A. 2013 'Developing competencies of supply chain
     professionals in Australia: Collaboration between businesses, universities
     and industry associations', *Supply Chain Management: An International
     Journal* 18.4: 429–39; Faems, D., Van Looy, B., and Debackere, K. 2005
     'Interorganizational collaboration and innovation: Toward a portfolio
     approach', *Journal of Product Innovation Management* 22.3: 238–50

8   Monk, G. 2007 'Collaborations with the dead', in Scott Thurston, ed,
     The Salt Companion to Geraldine Monk (pp. 178–87), Cambridge: Salt
     Publishing

Interviewer's Introduction

On échoue toujours de parler de ce qu'on aime (one always fails in speaking of what one loves).[1] This was the title of Roland Barthes's last piece of writing, found on a sheet of paper in his typewriter after his unexpected death.

Re-reading these interviews from 2013 to 2015 with some of Australia's most important and most interesting poets, I am struck by how close each one comes to speaking purely and profoundly about what they love, but not quite arriving at what I sense they might want to say. Each poet in this book of interviews talks about what is most important in their lives, what is most difficult, and what is most elusive, and there is a fascination in witnessing them, as it were, turn by turn, try to do this when put on the spot by their interviewer. It is like some kind of villanelle-world where the rounds of questions swirl in different ways through each encounter as the larger poem of these interviews unfolds for the reader. The interviews were not intended to have this effect, but placing them here against each other, so that we can witness how each poet tackles more or less the same questions, and how each differs from the other, it becomes something like a dance among the poets.

Each interview, I think, fails—not because of what the poets say, but because these interviews are constrained conversations. Again and again the interviewer brings the talk back to a schedule of questions. Though we forewarned each poet with a printed list of questions, it is evident from the following interview transcripts that these are very much spoken answers, they are a record of thinking on-the-wing, words tumbled out into the air and sometimes failing, sometimes managing to fly briefly, and always with the ring of conviction that important matters lie here.

Each transcript succeeds in bringing a distinctive voice to the preoccupations that drive these interviews. There is, for instance, the ceaselessly curious talk of Michael Sharkey; Jennifer Harrison's exquisitely

6

precise reflections; Diane Fahey's voice so alive with observations (even of what is happening on the roof of her house as the interview proceeds); Robyn Rowland's irrepressible duende combined with her social commitments; Ron Pretty's willingness to open his crafty perfection to the occasional accident; Mike Ladd speaking from his border zones; Ken Bolton enjoying talking behind the world's back; and Jill Jones juggling the virtual entity that is language with the music of her moods. Then there's Justin Clemens tripping over paradoxes wherever he turns, and Philip Salom being the consummate feeling-intellectual, living the life, perhaps, that Barthes was trying to construct for himself in the end by unlearning all that academia had taught him.

Reading these interviews, you might wonder why the interviewers didn't just let the poets talk and allow broader conversations to develop as they would. Why this schedule of questions? To answer that, it's necessary to say that these interviews are the byproduct of a research project spanning the years 2012 to 2016. The research project was funded by the Australian Research Council as a Discovery Project, with the title 'Understanding Creative Excellence: a case study in poetry'. The over-arching question for us was, 'What are the conditions, contexts and practices that lead to excellence in the writing of poetry?' Beyond the case study of poetry, though, the project aimed at producing useful insights into the practices and contexts for the work of successfully creative individuals. These are poets we have been interviewing, but they are also for the purposes of the project, examples of professionally creative individuals. Such concerns, then, shaped our questions.

The interviews selected for publication are a small Australian snapshot of the data we collected. In all, we interviewed seventy-six English-speaking poets from Australia, New Zealand, Singapore, Republic of South Africa, USA, Canada, Ireland, Scotland and England. The interviews collected here offer a lively picture of the ferment going on in Australian poetry, and the thinking, the struggles, and some of the issues dominating creative lives in the contemporary world. If you have ever wondered how poets become poets, how they actually write poetry, where they find the time to do it, how they justify doing this, and whether they identify as poets, then these interviews will offer you a handful of very different answers.

If the poets do fail, finally, in speaking adequately, genuinely, definitively, of what they love, it is only because no one can have the final word on such complex and open-ended matters.

Kevin Brophy

NOTES

1 Lotringer, S. 2011 'Barthes after Barthes', *Frieze*, 1 January 2011. Available at: https://frieze.com/article/barthes-after-barthes (accessed August 2018)

Prologue

The intimate link between *poetry* and *creativity* lies in front of us, there in the word itself: 'poetry' coming from the Ancient Greek verb *poiein*, which means 'to make' or 'to create'. Originally introduced to distinguish the writing of a song from the singing of it,[1] the Greek term quickly took on all-too-familiar connotations: the myth of the solitary poet, compelled to write in a fit of fevered creation, because possessed by a divine vision. True poetic creativity, that is, was *extra*ordinary—its source was beyond or outside the world of the ordinary, the everyday. Thus reads the myth. The stories told by the ten poets interviewed in this collection, however, reveal something quite different. The poets here are inspired not by the breath of divinities from outside the world, but by what lies before us all. In reading these interviews, we come to see that poetic creativity emerges from a vividly living awareness that, as Chesterton describes, 'this world is a wild and startling place'[2]—an awareness of the profundity of the ordinary and the everyday.

The myth of the divine nature of poetic creativity is a story that has been told many times before; here let me illustrate it by way of some brief remarks on two key texts in that story—one ancient, one modern. My first text is Plato's dialogue *Ion* (written c. 380BCE). Here, Socrates sums up the key elements of the Ancient Greek tradition—the story

9

of the poetic *enthousiasmós* (or, in the more familiar Latin, the *furor poeticus*)—in a beautiful speech:

> As the worshipping Corybantes are not in their senses when they dance, so the poets are not in their senses when they make these lovely lyric poems. No, when once they launch into harmony and rhythm, they are seized with the Bacchic transport and are possessed . . . For the poets tell us, don't they, that the melodies they bring us are gathered from rills that run with honey, out of glens and gardens of the Muses, and they bring them as the bees do honey, flying like the bees. And what they say is true, for a poet is a light and winged thing, and holy, and never able to compose until he has become inspired, and is beside himself, and reason is no longer in him . . . [For] not by art [*technê*] do they utter these, but by power divine . . . [Hence] it is not they who utter these precious revelations while their mind is not within them, but it is the god himself who speaks, and through them becomes articulate to us . . . [Thus] poems are not of human workmanship, but are divine and from the gods, and the poets are nothing but interpreters of the gods, each one possessed by the divinity to whom he is in bondage. (534a–e)[3]

Here, in Socrates's ironic presentation, are all the key features of the myth of poetic creativity. A true poem is not the result of the exercise of ('merely human') talents and capacities—as Socrates puts it in the passage above, poetry is 'not by *technê*' (the Greek term which lies at the root of such English words as 'technique' and 'technology'). Rather, poetry is produced through the poet's possession by something that comes from outside the commonplace world—'by power divine', provided by the Muses or the gods. In consequence, the poem itself is not, in strict sense, the ('merely human') words of the poet at all; rather, the divine presence speaks *through* the poet.

My second example of the poetic myth is one of the foundational texts of European Romanticism—and that which launched the 18th century cult of 'genius'—Edward Young's *Conjectures on Original Composition* (1759).[4] In this short but profoundly influential work, Young distinguishes sharply between those poetic works that are *imitations* and those that are genuinely *original*. In a deliberate echo of the Greek distinction between that produced by *technê* and that produced by 'power divine', Young argues that learned skills and capacities can only produce poetic works that are imitative. This is because to be skilled or learned is to be able to produce *according to rule*, and rule-following, by necessity, can only produce imitations—it is not creative. To be genuinely creative—to produce poetic works that are original—requires something of an altogether different order from mere learning (technique, skill, etc.). Namely, it requires *genius*, which establishes new rules by sheer force of example. To cite two famous passages from Young's work:

> An Original may be said to be of a vegetable nature; it rises spontaneously, from the vital root of genius; it grows, it is not made: Imitations are often a sort of manufacture wrought up by those mechanics, art, and labour, out of pre-existent materials not their own. (p. 7)

> Genius differs from a good understanding as a magician from a good architect; that raises his structure by means invisible; this by the skilful use of common tools. Hence genius has ever been supposed to partake of something divine. *Nemo unquam vir magnus fuit, sine aliquo afflatu divino [No-one was ever great without some divine inspiration (lit. 'breath')]*. Learning, destitute of this superior aid, is fond, and proud, of what has cost it much pains; is a great lover of rules, and boaster of famed examples. (p. 13)

Here, in Young's contribution to the myth of poetic creativity, we can see a restatement of the thought that original poems are the spontaneous overflowings of the inspired genius; they are not the result of labour, practice, skill, discipline, technique, painstaking work. We should also note a significant implication of Young's argument: that the genuinely creative poet must be, in an artistic sense, a *lone* figure, rather than embedded in a mutually-influencing community of other poets, readers, publishers, and critics. Because of Young's dichotomous split between 'originals' and 'imitations', any such relations of influence threaten to render the poet a mere imitator, manufacturing their poems 'out of pre-existent materials not their own'. In contrast, the originality of poetic genius is divine precisely in that, like God, it creates its works *ex nihilo*.

This myth of poetic creativity—illustrated in the two examples above—is, of course, a deep part of poetry's self-conception (at least in the 'Western' tradition). We are all familiar—probably *too* familiar—for example, with the story of how Coleridge's 'Kubla Khan' was 'a vision in a dream', eagerly written down in a passion of inspiration, until this was interrupted by an importunate person from Porlock. Blake wrote his poetry from the inspiration supposedly provided by mystical visions. Shelley insisted that poetry had a divine origin, writing that a poem 'is the creation of actions according to the unchangeable forms of human nature, as existing in the mind of the Creator, which is itself the image of all other minds'.[5] The mature poetry of W. B. Yeats had its origins in occult sessions of 'Automatic Script', where the pen was supposedly moved to write by the actions of other-worldly spirits. Even such a modern figure as Robert Graves is happy to claim that true poetry must be 'an unaccountable product of a trance'.[6] Such examples could easily be multiplied; they all testify to the enduring attraction of the myth of poetic inspiration as extraordinary and external—beyond human.

Let us now imagine a counter-myth. What would such a counter-myth look like? The myth of poetic creativity posits a cleavage between the truly *poetic* use of language, on the one hand, and the ordinary, the everyday, the 'merely human' use of language, on the other. Poetry (so says the myth) is language use founded in genius, the divine capacity to create from nothing—words used in ways that are altogether new, fresh, living, and unprecedented. In contrast, the ordinary use of language is mere imitation and rule-following; saying what has been said before: words that have rolled in countless mouths, and that, consequently, are dead, clichéd, and stale. The counter-myth we imagine here denies this cleavage. Poetry is not outside 'ordinary' language use; poetry is *inside* the ordinary, running through it like a golden thread.

All uses of language—no matter how apparently trivial or obvious—partake of the condition of poetry. This is because all uses of language involve extending words into new contexts, and this always involves the creative imagination. Poetry, that is, draws on our fundamental capacities to respond to the world, and to bring it to words—capacities that are deeply ordinary and everyday, though no less profound for that.

In constructing the genealogy of our counter-myth, let Immanuel Kant be its first spokesperson. Kant, with his democratic and republican spirit, despised the idea that any human capacity could have its source in some extra-worldly source of inspiration that spoke only to the privileged few—seeing in that idea the tap root of dogmatism and authoritarianism. The idea that poetry could come from 'an immediate and extraordinary communion with a higher nature'[7] is, in other words, an example of what Kant contemptuously termed *Schwärmerei* (variously translated as *enthusiasm*, or *fanaticism*). Instead, in his epoch-making *Critique of Pure Reason* (1781),[8] Kant makes the crucial argument that the creative imagination was not a special faculty, reserved only for special people (poets, artists), or used only during special activities (such as the writing of poetry). Rather, creative imagination—the 'productive synthesis of the imagination' (see esp. A118-122)—was an essential part of *every* thought, *every* judgment. The capacity to integrate that flash of black tail, that rustle in the agapanthus, with our past memories and our future anticipations, in a unified space and time, and thereby think that *the cat is in the garden*, is an astounding feat of imagination. It is precisely, for Kant, that creative, imaginative capacity that lies at the foundation of the human capacity to articulate our experience in thought and in language.

Kant called this capacity the 'productive imagination' because, he insisted, it is not mere rule-following—it is *creative*. Edward Young would have it that most of us—those not blessed with 'genius', at least—are mere imitators, slavish rule-followers; our thoughts and language use essentially the working of a mechanism or algorithm. It is the poetic geniuses alone who can forge new, fresh uses of words. For Kant, on the other hand, every thought, every use of language, has, at its heart, a *spontaneity*; indeed, the productive imagination just *is* spontaneity (B152), and 'it is because of this spontaneity that I call myself an *intelligence*' (B158n). In other words, that creativity which Young locates as outside the ordinary, Kant locates as inside it—as, indeed, its condition of possibility. If all thinking, all language use, did not partake of the condition of poetry, then there would be no thought and no language at all.

This Kantian thought we can find echoed in the later work of Wittgenstein. The *Philosophical Investigations*[9] is, among other things, a sustained attack on the idea that language use could ever be completely fixed and determined by rules—that speaking a language could be 'operating a calculus according to definite rules' (§81). Wittgenstein wants us to see that what ultimately underpins language use is spontaneous human activity. Hence his fondness for quoting Goethe's line from *Faust*: '*Im Anfang war die Tat*' ('In the beginning was the deed'; see, e.g., *On Certainty*, §402).[10] The relevance of this to our understanding of poetry is brought out clearly in the following passage in which Stanley Cavell summarises this key teaching of Wittgenstein's later philosophy:

> If what can be said in a language is not everywhere determined by rules, nor its understanding anywhere secured through universals, and if there are always new contexts to be met, new needs, new relationships, new objects, new perceptions to be recorded and shared, then perhaps it as true of a master of a language as of his apprentice that though 'in a sense' we learn the meaning of words and what objects are, the learning is never over, and we keep finding new potencies in words and new ways in which objects are disclosed.[11]

Or, as Derrida puts it, 'it is because writing is *inaugural*, in the fresh sense of the word, that it is dangerous and anguishing. It does not know where it is going'.[12] We are therefore, as Hemingway noted, always an apprentice and never a master.[13]

This is the sense in which, as I have suggested in the counter-myth sketched above, all language use—no matter how 'commonplace'—partakes of the condition of poetry. Fundamentally, poetry is about bringing the world and our experience to words—fresh words; words extended inaugurally into new contexts. Yet, as the philosophers mentioned above argue, *every* use of language involves the extension of words into new contexts in ways that exceed any 'rules' we could state, and is thereby a creative act. In the words of Cavell (quoted above), 'we keep finding new potencies in words and new ways in which objects are disclosed'. All contexts are thus, in an important sense, new and all words are, in this sense, fresh.

The myth of poetic creativity posits a sharp cleavage between poetry and so-called 'ordinary' uses of language; our counter-myth instead emphasises the continuities that exist between them. In doing this, it could sound to some ears as if I am suggesting that everyone is a poet, and that every use of language is poetry. But I am trying to emphasise—against the culturally powerful myth that exalts the true poet as a divinely inspired genius—that poetry in fact draws deeply from the well of the everyday and the ordinary. Of course, poetry involves a heightening and intensifying—perhaps one could call it a *purifying*—of the creative spontaneity that is the condition of possibility of all language use.

This is brought out clearly by the ten interviews with poets collected in this book. What is their 'muse', the source of their inspiration? What moves them to write? The poets here do not wait to be filled by the breath of some divinity; they are not Young's mythical 'geniuses' who create something from nothing. They are writing to what is in front of them—what is in front of all of us; the commonplace. They write from friendships and loves and enmities; from travel and places both strange and familiar; their poems come from the most ordinary of experiences: seeing birds on a rooftop; the pain of a toothache; a new baby; a glass of wine; a school teacher reading a poem to a class; the feel of a fountain pen on smooth paper; the faces of the audience at a reading; domesticity; darkness; silence. Not only this, but we should note the importance of *technê* in their remarks—their poems are not the effortless productions of the mythical 'genius'. All of the poets interviewed emphasise, in their varied ways, the importance of disciplined work and technical knowledge. Writing poetry, like all human skills, involves such commonplace things as practice and repetition (writing and rewriting), discipline, experience, care, learned skills in rhythm and metre. The poetic creativity displayed by all these poets is not a mysterious bestowal from another world; it is, in a profound sense, ordinary.

Monica Carroll

NOTES

1   Ford, A. 2002 *The Origins of Criticism: Literary Criticism and Poetic Theory in Classical Greece*, Princeton: Princeton University Press, p. 131

2   Chesterton, G. K. 1908 *Orthodoxy*, London: William Clowes & Sons, ch. 4

3   Plato, *Ion* in Burnet, J., ed 1922 *Platonis Opera*, Vol. 3, Oxford: Oxford University Press. Translation based loosely on that by L. Cooper in Hamilton, E., and Cairns, H., eds 1961 *The Collected Dialogues of Plato*, Princeton: Princeton University Press

4   Young, E. 1918 *Conjectures on Original Composition*, edited by E. J. Morley, London: Longmans, Green and Co

5   Shelley, P. B. 1998 'A Defense of Poetry' in D. Wu, ed., *Romanticism: An Anthology* (pp. 944–56), Oxford: Blackwell

6   Graves, R. 1969 *On Poetry: Collected Talks and Essays*, New York: Doubleday, p. 286

7   Kant, I. 2007 'Observations on the feeling of the beautiful and sublime' (trans P. Guyer) in *Anthropology, History, and Education*, edited by G. Zöller and R. B. Louden, *Cambridge Edition of the Works of Immanuel Kant*, Cambridge: Cambridge University Press, p. 251n

8   Kant, I. 1998 *Critique of Pure Reason*, translated and edited by P. Guyer and
    A. W. Wood, *Cambridge Edition of the Works of Immanuel Kant*, Cambridge:
    Cambridge University Press
9   Wittgenstein, L. 1967 *Philosophische Untersuchungen / Philosophical
    Investigations*. Trans G. E. M. Anscombe, Oxford: Blackwell
10 Wittgenstein, L. 1975 *Über Gewissheit / On Certainty*. Trans D. Paul and G.
    E. M. Anscombe, Oxford: Blackwell
11 Cavell, S. 1979 *The Claim of Reason: Wittgenstein, Skepticism, Morality and
    Tragedy*, Oxford: Oxford University Press, p. 180
12 Derrida, J. 1978 'Force and signification' in *Writing and Difference*. Trans A.
    Bass, London: Routledge, p. 11
13 Hemingway, E. 1961 Interview, *New York Journal-America*, 11 July

"Out of that came a great love of birds"
Diane Fahey

Clifton Springs, Victoria

KEVIN: What do you feel are your points of connection to the world? Which connections matter to you?

DIANE: My connections with family and lifelong friends have, of course, mattered very much. These days I also have some friends who share an interest in mindfulness meditation, and quite a few who are poets. I have the example of the work of other poets, past and present; and belief in poetry itself. Poetry is such a wonderful thing to have in one's life; it's a sustaining and potentially healing, transforming force.

KEVIN: Do you think that poetry separates you from the world as much as it connects you to the world?

DIANE: To some extent, yes. My lifestyle involves a lot of solitude, but I mostly don't feel isolated. Isolation is an experience of lack and of absence, and takes a lot of energy to work through, whereas solitude can involve an awareness of presence—of being present to oneself and to the world—and so be quite nourishing. I also believe in balancing things out, because prolonged separateness can lead to distorted viewpoints: one needs to find the middle way between self and other, inner and outer. I have long phases of doing my own thing and then I connect with friends, go down to Melbourne to visit art galleries, et cetera.

KEVIN: Can you remember when you first encountered poetry?

DIANE: There would have been nursery rhymes, bouncy and strange, giving that sense of language permeated by pattern and rhythm in a beautiful primal way—an early imprinting. At school I remember in Grade 6 our homework was to learn parts of poems by heart and there would be an oral test after lunch. Almost everyone would fail, including me. It was an experience of getting those rhythms and patterns into your bones, getting it into your ear and into your physical being. I remember, in secondary school, some very good poetry teaching, including of Shakespeare. One particular memory is of Brian Vrepont's 'Grape Harvest',[1] which was in our anthology. The teacher, Miss Kearney, broke it down, analysing different elements and then we took down by dictation a page-long appreciation of the poem. That was a wonderful experience.

KEVIN: That's a more self-conscious appreciation of poetry than the primer experience.

DIANE: That's right. You become more conscious of the elements that compose it. Around that time I won a prize for writing a poem about Our Lady that was supposed to be in the school magazine, except the nuns locked the completed magazine away in the convent. There must have been something in it they didn't like.

KEVIN: How much poetry do you read now and how regularly?

DIANE: A lot, almost every day. I've been reading Mary Oliver for many years, and Rumi. Jane Kenyon, Kathleen Jamie, and Ted Kooser: he's a lovely US poet. And some Irish poets: Moya Cannon, Michael Longley, the Donegal poet Francis Harvey, who has now left us, and many others. I love the early Chinese poets, especially Du Fu.

KEVIN: If you were to describe yourself to a stranger, would you identify yourself as a poet and would you identify yourself as a *kind* of poet?

DIANE: I try to avoid doing that because in Australia poetry doesn't really mean much to most people. So mentioning it seems to create problems sometimes. And, of course, many people write and are interested in poetry. To claim the role as a vocation feels awkward, although that is, for me, the reality.

KEVIN: I guess the next question often is, what kind of poet are you?

DIANE: Lyric poetry is important to me, but I'm not primarily a lyric poet. I've written poems on myths and fairy tales, the natural world, my personal story, and social and political issues.

KEVIN: Do you see a coherence, or is it scattered?

DIANE: I don't see it as scattered. I do see it as coherent because the personal poetry I wrote—which was, to some extent, against my own instinct, because I'm a very private person—was spurred on by Jung's idea of the individuation process: that you have to discover and work with your story and create your story as you live.[2] That took me to myths and fairy tales, which constitute such an extraordinary world of stories that say so much to us about our psychological, emotional and spiritual pathways. I came into nature writing after an early life of being an urban person, growing up in a South Melbourne terrace house; as my life has unfolded I've become more attuned to nature and therefore written on natural settings, birds and other creatures.

That itself becomes an interesting journey because you don't want to say the obvious or be simply descriptive; you have to work out a process, a way of being and relating to things in the natural world. Out of that came a great love of birds, which is inexhaustible, it's all inexhaustible. The world is so full of inspiring and beguiling creatures and environments.

I was out in the backyard the other day, hanging out the washing. Sitting on next-door's roof, which seems to be the setting of a social club for birds, there were two rainbow lorikeets. One was tending itself, preening, and the other spontaneously joined in at the back of its companion's neck, presumably attending to a place that was unreachable. This went on for a long time and it was spontaneous co-operation and support. It was just wonderful. I have to stop myself writing about birds at times because there is so much to say, and yet you can't talk about birds all the time. But it is a passion.

KEVIN: Maybe a passion is what coheres it all?

DIANE: I'd say my passion as a poet is a search for connection and for a rounded, rich sense of life that is true to the difficult aspects of life.

KEVIN: What about politics? Do politics come into your poetry?

DIANE: Increasingly, I'm thinking about the nature of violence and the relationship between absolute power and murder; and it's hard to miss the mindless infliction of suffering in many settings, sometimes at the hands of the powerless. Where are we coming from with all this?— what is the cause of such widespread failures of basic human awareness? I would like to explore these themes in future work, though in general it seems wisest to do this in pinhole glimpses, or by indirection, rather than imaginatively re-entering trauma and violation. However, this year I wrote a poem called, 'A Death in Winter',[3] inspired by the death of a Tamil Sri Lankan man, Leo Seemanpillai, in Geelong; I wanted to record the depradations of torture and repression he had known, and to honour him as a person, and contribute to the way he is remembered.

An early book, *Metamorphoses*,[4] looked at the feminist issue of the imbalance of power between men and women, and the consequent enmeshment in a web of violence and violation. A second book also based on figures in Greek mythology, *Listening to a Far Sea*,[5] attempted to rebalance the relationship—that is, to access images of creativity and reconciliation in order to avoid getting stuck in a polarising dynamic. In *The Wing Collection*,[6] the poem the title alludes to was inspired by the psychic ethos of capitalism. It ended with a man trying on wings as if you could buy everything, as if you could buy transcendence. What is portrayed is an ultimate loneliness.

KEVIN: How does moving affect your writing?

DIANE: Earlier in my life I lived in England. It was important to take my bearings in another culture. Travel challenges you to look at your ingrained assumptions; it's a great learning experience. My focus now is mainly on Ireland; I feel deeply at home when I'm there. I don't believe in idealising Ireland, but I have found it has drawn a deep creative response and fed my poetry in ways that were very powerful. I've started three books there, for instance.

KEVIN: Do you go back to the same place in Ireland each time?

DIANE: No. I've covered different kinds of ground. I haven't set eyes on the north-west coast, which I hope to do next year, when I'll be researching and writing a book on the west of Ireland.

KEVIN: You don't feel the same urge to discover parts of Australia?

DIANE: Later in my life, I would like to do much more of that.

KEVIN: I suppose there's a wholly different task and challenge to travelling in Australia because the population is comparatively sparse and, for non-Indigenous people, the deepest and oldest layers of their cultures of origin, of their first heritage and history, are not present, and the distances are enormous, whereas in Ireland, all those things are reversed.

DIANE: Yes, that's true. Ireland's a complex culture with, of course, a lot of damaged people in its population, just as Australia has; but I find the supportive and welcoming nature of many Irish people to be especially heartening. I think it has been, and still is in large degree, a very communal culture where people are aware of others in a close, perceptive way. There's a sense of being recognised as a person in deep ways, and that's a lovely experience.

KEVIN: You lived in England for a while?

DIANE: That's right. I did a lot of poetry courses, met other poets and concentrated on poetry. I found friendships and inspirations there that helped me to develop as a poet. It was also a personal quest and

I also did a lot of psychological courses and followed various spiritual interests.

KEVIN: So location is less important to you than the fact that you bring yourself and your passions and your interests to wherever you are.

DIANE: Yes. I'm fortunate to feel sustained by the place I'm in now, and have truly settled here. It's often been difficult to adapt and translate myself physically into a new milieu, but you follow a quest to find certain things in people, in yourself, and in your own and other cultures. That's what motivates you to travel, to explore new settings. All those stored experiences can later be harvested, so one hopes, in various ways.

* * *

KEVIN: Coming back to education and those first encounters with poetry and school, how did your education shape you?

DIANE: At the University of Melbourne I studied literature and there were certain poems that struck great sparks. I can remember reading Yeats's 'Sailing to Byzantium'[7] and Emily Dickinson's 'Further in Summer than the Birds',[8] Robert Frost's 'Stopping by Woods on a Snowy Evening'.[9] They became touchstones, they became indelible. Poems that entrance you and draw you out of yourself. They possess a completeness, but they're elusive. You feel the voice of the life of the poet speaking through such poems.

KEVIN: And without that university experience, you wouldn't have become the kind of poet you've become?

DIANE: That's an interesting question. If it's so deep in you, will you find a way later on in life? The exposure to poets, poetry, good poetry teaching, wonderful anthologies, created a journey into poetic vision and literature generally. It would have been harder in those days to find your way into further education or creative writing courses, but in a culture where that is much more possible now, many people find their way and get what they need to develop their creativity.

KEVIN: Were you aiming towards a working life, a career of any kind at that time?

DIANE: I thought of myself as becoming a teacher. I did teach during some parts of my life. But back then, I was contending with difficulties which made that path seem too demanding. I had become depressed from the end of school, and that continued for many years. So that was the backdrop of my being at Melbourne University. It complicated my life and I ended up not feeling I could have a role in society or do work. I was clinically depressed for a quite a number of years, and was more or less 'outside', and I didn't know what possibilities were there for me. Becoming a poet was a terrifically important thread, though it is, of course, not a way of earning a living. And you can't write poetry all the time because it's so intense. But you make it part of your life, and that helped me greatly.

KEVIN: And what about your relationship then to other poets? Did you move out into a professional and collegial world of poets?

DIANE: In England, in the 1980s, I used to go to the Poetry Society readings. There was a sense of a small community there, and you heard interesting well-known people, and newer poets. And I went to some Arvon courses; they were just starting then, but they're now well established. You live for five days in the country with twelve or so other participants, and two writers who act as mentors. I went to a number of those courses, and they were often transforming experiences. I remember showing one of the writers a poem I'd written about Ophelia, from my first book. He asked, *what would Ophelia really have felt?* then, *go for a walk and see what happens.* So I went for a walk and most of the poem, which is called 'Remembering Ophelia',[10] came to me on that walk. I didn't have any pencil and paper. I got back and my team was cooking the evening meal. I was supposed to be cooking stew and I hid because I had to write the poem down. I lost a couple of sections, but I got down the twelve that eventually became the poem—but then I had to deal with the consequence of my intransigence! It was a very creative challenge, very direct, saying, *go out there and get it.* That can unlock people.

KEVIN: Were any of those connections you made with people there permanent or long lasting?

DIANE: They were, yes. I was in a group with two other women poets, Linda Saunders and Pam Gillilan, who has now passed away; that was a close and enduring friendship. I've always found those small groups of poets very helpful.

KEVIN: And is that process continuing with any other poets? Do you show your work to others?

DIANE: I've worked with Katherine Gallagher, who lives in London but returns to Australia, Sandy Fitts in Melbourne and Rosemary Blake, who lives in Geelong—all poets. The chemistry works well if you're happy for people to say, *this line isn't working* or *I don't understand what you mean.* We might think we've said something, but we haven't really; or other people might read it quite differently. Working with poetry, you're continually seeing new possibilities and if you're prepared to tear up the ticket and try something different, all kinds of new possibilities are released.

It becomes an extension of the creative process. The process of sharing often becomes a dialogue in which you are finding the solutions yourself as well as being offered ideas by another person. If it's a trusting friendship that's working as a two-way thing, that can happen. Otherwise you just have to work at it by yourself over time, but it takes much longer.

KEVIN: Could you characterise the kinds of effects you would like to have on your readers?

DIANE: The love of poetry as a reader has brought me insight, a deeper engagement with experience, and touchstones. If I can offer a reader any of those things, then that is, on one level, the fulfilment of the poem. I find both great challenge and great solace in different kinds of poetry. In Mary Oliver's 'The Summer Day',[11] she writes, *Tell me, what is it you plan to do / with your one wild and precious life?* That is a touchstone question.

* * *

KEVIN: How do you find the words to do your bidding?

DIANE: Sometimes in the act of saying things we end up at a different place. Surprise is a crucial element of poetry: we have to move into a new place, we need to surprise ourselves. That's one of the things that creativity does, it brings in something new that's not expected. It's a question of proceeding in a way that will allow that to happen.

KEVIN: Do you use material from conversations, overheard speech? And how do you feel about doing that kind of thing?

DIANE: I've written portraits of people seen in the street or met briefly. 'True Confessions'[12] is a sequence about different women I saw in the street when I lived near Hampstead in London. They were homeless or outsider people. I wouldn't expect any of them ever to see the poems I wrote about them, but I didn't feel right in myself about it. There are a few poems like that—where I may be on the money but I don't know what right I've got to enter another person's reality, what's carried within their depths. That's their secret. So I turned away from those sorts of poems.

I've written a lot about my mother and father, but that's in a special space and it's got an intention of honouring, telling the truth but honouring what they have given or who they were.

KEVIN: You showed them those poems?

DIANE: They saw ones that I wrote earlier on. I wrote a sequence about my father recovering from illness, 'Poem of Thanksgiving'.[13] That was important to me because I won what is now called the Newcastle

Poetry Prize. That brought me home from England. I'd been in England for many years and I didn't know how to come back or when to come back. But it triggered my return at a time when I needed to help my parents, with whom I lived while my father was recovering from one major operation, then waiting to undergo another. At that stressful time, I would often go out into nature, into the environment of Barwon Heads, walking, looking, recording details. That was partly the seed of my becoming a nature writer. Now I'm writing a book about my mother. It's very searching on a personal level, but I feel okay with it and believe she would be okay with it, too. When I wrote *The Mystery of Rosa Morland*[14] I enjoyed a holiday from the whole thing of talking about actual people because I was making up people set in an imagined, invented world, and removed from that problem of accessing the deeply personal.

KEVIN: Do you have to be in the right mood to compose? Or is it a matter of no mood?

DIANE: I would say there are times when I deliberately set out to write a new work. I don't have to have a conscious theme or focus. If I'm in a difficult place I often write a stream of consciousness and see what is triggered from it. Almost always something can create movement and that can trigger a tapping into unconscious material or memory that's going to be helpful or ask to be written about.

KEVIN: And do you do that writing by hand?

DIANE: At that stage, yes. And in the ordinary rhythms of my life, when I'm reflecting or out walking, looking at the sea or at birds, lines and fragments may come that I build on later. I jot them down on bits of paper, which I put in a pile. It's chaotic. Mood doesn't come into it much, but an attentive state can be important. Or if one is under duress, that will create pressure, which may provoke or unlock images and creative ideas.

KEVIN: Does music play a role?

DIANE: I never listen to music while I'm working. Poetry and music are such powerful pathways that I can't combine attentiveness to them at once. Great music, like great poetry, is enthralling and can invoke a sense of the ineffable wholeness of life, even while permeated by a sense of conflict and pain. Turning on the radio and randomly hearing a Beethoven symphony or concerto by chance can be a staggering surprise, even though one knows it so well. The power and courage of his encounter with life, his sense of beauty, are communicated with an incredible immediacy. Recently I had a great experience listening to *Fantasia on a Theme by Thomas Tallis*, by Vaughan Williams.[15] Again, its completeness, its containing so many opposites in a dynamic way . . . there's an extraordinary sense of beauty and of pain that is both majestic and poignant. A completeness, even while the music is constantly changing and evolving. Poetry can do that as well.

KEVIN: When you listen to music do you put that time aside to listen to music?

DIANE: I don't often sit down and listen to music as such. But, as a background to the day, when I'm doing practical tasks, or driving, I listen to Classic FM—you get a wonderful range of music there, as well as revisiting some of the extraordinary peak experiences within the Western tradition of music that I know best. There can be the revisiting of a piece I haven't heard for decades, or the impact of something quite new, drawn from a musical culture I'm not familiar with. The frontiers of art forms are ever-evolving, so new relationships and possibilities emerge, new settings and new interpretations—this is a living process.

*   *   *

KEVIN: How quickly do you write?

DIANE: At times I've written very quickly. Now I've got a lot of patience, in evolving a poem, getting ideas down and developing them. A friend said, *you've got to try and get it all down straight away.*

It's like recording a dream—you get down as much as you can before it fades; the thoughts and images may be quite fragmentary, but are potentially very valuable. Working on a poem can take a really long time. Most of the poems in my current book, *A House by the River*,[16] are over a decade old. I'm still working on them.

KEVIN: What do you do with the drafts as you move from one draft to another?

DIANE: It's easier now to archive one's own drafts, as it were, because of filing them on a computer. But I do have stacks and stacks of paper drafts from earlier years; and I still do a lot of printouts of poems in progress. There are folders of poems all around this house; in some moods they feel like the bane of my life! No system can stave off chaos, but of course we have to try. It's important to try. I want to throw most of my manuscripts away, but I can't release them yet. I've got to find a place in myself where I can let them go.

KEVIN: So what about the difference between composing and editing: are they a similar process for you or are they very different? As you move from one into the other?

DIANE: At an early stage I'll start writing alternative words or phrases around parts of lines in a draft. Editing almost finished poems can involve breaking them open in radical ways. You end up rewriting parts, which is very difficult because one is trying to create an organic whole with interconnections and levels happening, dynamically. If you interfere with part of that working arrangement that can create a big problem. With some poems I will just go back to that one problem, day after day. I don't know if it's too much to say that there's a kind of Zen involved. You're listening and waiting, then you take up the poem again, and then you step back again, and then you return . . . At times it feels like you're allowing time to do the work, or your unconscious—which I think is partly true.

KEVIN: Would you say you're a poet who depends upon the stanza break to shape and control a poem?

DIANE: I don't think so. The key thing for me in poetry is the shaping voice. But, of course, form is an essential part of the process of that voice animating and driving the poem, a further shaping. I am fascinated by poetic forms and have tried many approaches. Now I'm using the sonnet but in a different way, in a more relaxed way than in my previous book of sonnets, *Sea Wall and River Light.*[17] I'm modifying the form, breaking a few rules. Working with the sonnet feels more organic now, though the lines will still often fall into either 8/6, 6/8 or 7/7 stanzas. There are all these choices around developing a sonnet but it often does find a point of balance within itself between different movements. That's fascinating. And it's not simply that I'm imprinted with Shakespeare and other poets who mastered the sonnet: the form itself has its own dynamic.

Part of me wants a completeness, but the most important thing is being true to the process. Sometimes you've got to disrupt things, but you want that to be contained within the poem. Some people want disruption for its own sake, and that's a different thing.

KEVIN: Let's move onto the penultimate question. When you are writing, why do you stop writing, and how do you finish poems? And I think that's not just asking you what time of the day you stop writing.

DIANE: I tend not to go beyond the bounds of my energy now because it can take so long to recover from mental and creative exhaustion. So I mostly work slowly. I'm very intensive when I get going, but I've got to stop, otherwise I burn out. I can concentrate for hours, but I tend to break it up and do something physical. I walk up and down my driveway or walk down by the bay. It's like moving from one part of your being to another, and allowing the mind to recover its resources and establish your own completeness again. Being a writer is a physical thing, you have to attend to the body as well and respect your own resources.

I've always been a very driven person. Earlier in my life I was seeking desperate answers when I was dealing with depression. I'm less driven now, personally and creatively, because I have learnt to trust the processes more.

I would say that some poems are enjoyable to write and some are like puzzles or diversions. If you really want to drop the anchor—that is, plumb certain kinds of depths—you have to wait on the right energies and inner resources to carry that through. It's not just a matter of pressing onwards; it's a matter of waiting, or seeking and finding the right kind of inner space for the writing of the poem.

KEVIN: And a last final, strange question: is there anything your readers owe you?

DIANE: In a word, no. Language and experience are so diverse and multi-layered that different people will take different things from poems. Sometimes by carrying the story of a poem in myself, if it's taken many years to complete, it becomes woven into my life and a deep-memoried part of my experience. So, I have a certain way of understanding it, but I am interested in the insights and amplifications people bring when, say, I'm talking with a group in a poetry reading setting, or when I am offered responses from friends or colleagues in the poetry world. There can be very interesting interchanges from which fresh understandings arise. You feel the poem is in the world unfolding, rippling out, and intersecting with other sets of unfoldings and ripplings.

NOTES

1   Vrepont, Brian 1956 'Grape Harvest' from *The Boomerang Book of Australian Poetry*, edited by Enid Moodie, Heddle London: Longmans, Green & Co
2   For Carl Jung—in contrast to the Freudian approach, where the self emerges from the ego—the self precedes the ego, and can never be fully apprehended. Jung's individuation is the process of discovering that self, and becoming who one really is. See CG Jung, *Two Essays on Analytical Psychology*, trans FRC Hull, London: Routledge, 1966 [1935]
3   Fahey, Diane 2015 'A Death in Winter', *Eureka Street*, vol.25, no.5
4   Fahey, Diane 1988 *Metamorphoses*, Sydney: Dangaroo Press

5   Fahey, Diane 1998 *Listening to a Far Sea*, Alexandria: Hale and Iremonger

6   Fahey, Diane 2011 *The Wing Collection: New and Selected Poems*, Glebe:
     Puncher and Wattmann

7   Yeats, W B 1933 'Sailing to Byzantium' from *The Poems of W. B. Yeats: A
     New Edition*, edited by Richard J. Finneran, London: Macmillan

8   Dickinson, Emily 1866 'Further in Summer than the Birds', Fr 895, J 1068

9   Frost, Robert 1923 'Stopping by Woods on a Snowy Evening' from *The
     Poetry of Robert Frost*, edited by Edward Connery Lathem, New York: Henry
     Holt and Company

10 Fahey, Diane 1983 'Remembering Ophelia', from *Instructions for Honey Ants
     and Other Poems*, Newcastle: University of Newcastle

11 Oliver, Mary 1990 'The Summer Day', from *House of Light*, Boston: Beacon
     Press

12 Fahey, Diane 1986 'True Confessions', *Writing Women* vol. 5 no. 3

13 Fahey, Diane 1985 'Poem of Thanksgiving: On My Father's Recovery from
     Illness', from *Poem of Thanksgiving and Other Poems*, Newcastle: University
     of Newcastle

14 Fahey, Diane 2007 *The Mystery of Rosa Morland*, Thornbury: Clouds of
     Magellan

15 Williams, Ralph Vaughan 1910 *Fantasia on a Theme by Thomas Tallis*

16 Fahey, Diane 2002 'A House by the River' from *Unfamiliar Tides: The
     Newcastle Poetry Prize 2001/2002*, Newcastle: Newcastle City Council

17 Fahey, Diane 2006 *Sea Wall and River Light*, Carlton: Five Islands Press

"Look at the rasa of the poem"
Jennifer Harrison

University of Melbourne, Victoria

KEVIN: We start from the assumption that a poet is connected to the world. So, Jen, what are your points of connection to the world as a poet?

JENNIFER: I think it's an interesting question about whether you're connected with poetry to a social world, an intellectual world, or perhaps a private world. I see poetry as connecting me to those different spheres in differing ways. There's a connection to a social world through friends and colleagues and there's a connection to an intellectual world through thinking about poetry and reading about poetry and exploring a critique in our intellectual poetry understanding. There's the connection to a private world, which I think is to do with exploring one's own creativity. I work in psychiatric medicine, which is a practice of listening and being available to others. I find poetry connects me to my own creativity, maybe preferencing myself and what I feel and think over the listening to benefit others. There's quite a private world.

KEVIN: Something like an antidote to the professional work.

JENNIFER: A balance, I think. Antidote suggests that it drains something. I don't feel quite like that; I feel it's a different exploration that is not appropriate to, or not an opportunity given in, the other work.

KEVIN: What has kept you writing?

JENNIFER: I've always written. I had a first poem published when I was seven or eight in the *Sydney Morning Herald*. I've written since I was a child, not as in keeping a diary, but writing poetry or story writing. I've always had an interest in that area of practice.

KEVIN: What factors have sustained that practice?

JENNIFER: What I remember from childhood is the joy of creativity, the joy of the imagination. I found it pleasurable and fun. Perhaps some of that fun disappears later over the years, but I still recall the pleasure of writing story. I did quite well at school, so there was secondary reinforcement of doing well in those areas of study. We weren't a big family for books, it was more a sporting, practical family, but my mother did keep a little linen-covered poetry book. She'd read poems that she liked and she'd enter them in that book by hand. I have a strong memory of her pleasure in the poetry of that book, so I think that was an influence. Over the years, there was a long time when I didn't write much during medical training and psychiatric training; so there was a break pursuing other intellectual pursuits, but then I came back to it after I'd completed psychiatry training.

KEVIN: Can you remember first encountering poetry?

JENNIFER: Very clearly. In my mother's book. In primary school if we needed a poem for show and tell or some other kind of event, with my friends, I'd practise one of the poems from Mum's book and perform that at school.

KEVIN: Do you remember who some of the poets were?

JENNIFER: Henry Kendall's 'Bell-birds'[1] is the one I most clearly remember, but there were others. Quite a few had an emotional rhythmic aspect to the poetry. That, I think, attracted my mother. There were poems about the Foreign Legion and being lost in deserts, and poems about the second world war, but Henry Kendall's 'Bell-birds', is the one I remember most because of the absolutely beauty of the sounds in that poem.

KEVIN: And what happened to that book?

JENNIFER: I have it. She gave it to me a few years ago when she sold up her house and moved to a nursing home apartment.

KEVIN: So she understood how important it was.

JENNIFER: Yes, she kept it all her life.

*   *   *

KEVIN: When you introduce yourself to strangers, do you ever introduce yourself as a poet?

JENNIFER: Occasionally in context. To a stranger, no. To a stranger in a poetry context, I might, but I wouldn't bowl up and say, *hi I'm a poet.* It might be, *what do you do?* I would say, *I'm a poet.* In other contexts, perhaps less so.

KEVIN: When you do tell people that you're a poet, can you attach a descriptor to that, in terms of what kind of poet you are?

JENNIFER: No, never. People ask, *well what kind of poetry do you write?* I find that quite hard to discuss or clarify. I generally don't say what kind of poet I am; I feel it often comes from a non-poet perspective and not knowing what to say about poetry. I find people who don't write poetry sometimes struggle with that question more than I do, actually.

KEVIN: Yeah, it's an interesting question, isn't it, because it's a perfectly reasonable question to ask a musician, what kind of music they might write.

JENNIFER: Exactly, jazz or classical; exactly. But I don't think it's as clear. Often what underpins the question is, do you write rhyming poetry or not. It's hard to explain what sort of contemporary poetry you might know. So I usually say, if I'm asked that question, *I tend to* *write contemporary poetry*, and then they might ask about what sorts of topics interest me and I might talk about that.

KEVIN: On that question of topics, do you find that you use poetry to engage with social or political issues?

JENNIFER: When I started writing poetry as a teenager, after the childhood exuberance, I wrote a lot of poems about social issues sometimes about people less well off, or stigmatised etc. These days I tend less to engage overtly with social issues, although I do occasionally write a poem based on current events, particularly significant things that happen to women; then sometimes I'll be motivated to write politically.

KEVIN: Can you remember what the last one was?

JENNIFER: The last one was motivated by the rape and murder of Jill Meagher in Melbourne, near Sydney Road.[2] What prompted me to write that poem was how it affected my relationship with my daughter who was living alone in that area at the time, and our discussion about how she could protect herself when going out at night, and how indignant she became with that discussion, as in, *what am I supposed to do, not go out?* It was an interesting discussion. Often the social motivators intersect perhaps with more personal or more private ones.

KEVIN: Do you find that moving home and travelling have a big effect on what you write and how you write?

JENNIFER: I lived overseas for eleven years in early adult life and travelled extensively through those years. I lived in Asia, UK, New Zealand and Boston before returning to Australia. And some of that time was medical practice, some of that time was involved with writing poetry and the practice of creative writing. It didn't really influence my practice of writing. I think it influenced content more so. Perhaps I was able to become quite flexible: as a mother and a psychiatrist with limited time, I'm very flexible about where I write.

KEVIN: How has your education shaped the kind of poetry you write?

JENNIFER: I have a particular interest in German poetry. I studied German for my high school certificate in New South Wales. There were only two in the class, myself and Kim Grundy, Reg Grundy's daughter.[3] We used to travel into the city to go to classes together because it wasn't offered at the school. I loved the language and reading German literature. I read a lot of German poets at that time. It was something outside the school curriculum and it was fabulous and interesting.

KEVIN: Were you studying literature at the same time? At Year 12?

JENNIFER: Ah, in those days it was slightly different; you just studied English really, and literature was part of that; but English and literature have always been aspects of learning that I've enjoyed and been good at. When I moved on to study medicine, I was in the first year of a five-year course at the University of New South Wales, and they required you to do other subjects because they wanted doctors to be less insular. I took creative writing and wrote a short novel for that course while I was studying medicine. It was a great foresight, I think, to see that doctors need to have a varied extensive experience of study, not just a science one.

KEVIN: And what happened to that novel?

JENNIFER: I still have it. I never published it. I never went on to do anything with it, but it's an important piece of writing to me.

KEVIN: Has studying medicine and psychiatry shaped the poetry that you write?

JENNIFER: Definitely, in a few ways. It shaped the language I use, and shaped something that's deeper, more a poetic spirit or a sensibility. I think science study shaped some of my choices for poetry subjects as well. For instance, in *Cabramatta/Cudmirrah*,[4] for the Cudmirrah section I researched in depth the history of shells, marine biology and seaside geology. I probably wouldn't have approached a book of poems with quite that approach if I hadn't been schooled in a scientific discourse through medicine.

When training in psychiatry there's quite a lot of academic and conceptual reading in psychoanalysis and psychotherapy, particularly in child psychiatry. I remember when I was doing that training, we'd have four or five supervision sessions a week where you'd be exploring your own psychotherapy and transference in thinking at a deep level about language. One evening, rather suddenly when in the company of some friends after dinner I began to see language as vertical, as having multiple depths, depths that we probably haven't even understood. I began to feel the complexity of language as absolutely extraordinary, and I think psychoanalytic thinking brought that experience to the fore for me.

KEVIN: And is psychoanalysis at the core of your practice?

JENNIFER: No, not at all. I work in the field of autism and developmental disorders in children. I have a neuropsychiatric practice, but psychoanalytic thinking and psychotherapeutic understandings balance with a neuropsychiatry approach. It's an integrated approach.

KEVIN: What about the role that your relationships with other poets might play in affecting your practice, influencing your poetry?

JENNIFER: Well, I think there are other poets you read and poets you know personally, and they both have a significant effect. Probably the poets I read have more of an effect on my work than the poets who are my friends or even mentors. I often read a particular poet when I'm writing a book and immerse myself in their poetry. I've selected them for some reason, which is usually to do with the themes that I'm exploring, whether content or a particular poetic sensibility. I never find that I write like that poet in my poems, but there is something that I gain from immersing myself in their sensibility or their approach to topic.

KEVIN: Are there some poets you're reading now?

JENNIFER: I've been reading Tranströmer,[5] the Swedish poet. He has a psychology background and I find that there's a sensibility in his work that I relate to strongly.

KEVIN: Do you have people who read and comment on your drafts?

JENNIFER: There've been a couple of mentors, but very few. I've never been comfortable in poetry workshops. They don't suit my personality or practice, but I do like working with, perhaps, single people whose work I respect or who somehow are bringing something to my work that I'm not seeing. One of those has been Kevin Pearson, whom I happened to meet when he was starting his press in Melbourne. It was the most accidental and happy circumstance. He was a mentor very early on in shaping the first book I ever published. And then more recently I think, the poet Alex Skovron, and John Leonard the academic and anthologist.

KEVIN: That's interesting to me that it's three men.

JENNIFER: It is. In my generation of poetry making in Australia there has never been a woman poet in the generation above me that has made herself available or approached me in the way that those poets have. I've actually found poetry mentorship from the women in the generation above me a bit lacking. I wonder if it's because I'm new to Melbourne and I wasn't educated here; perhaps there's something in that, but I'm not sure.

KEVIN: When we read about Marianne Moore and Elizabeth Bishop,[6] I imagine Marianne Moore saw the potential and the opportunity to bring that potential on. That created its own complications, of course.

JENNIFER: Yes, and it might have been different if I'd studied academically at Melbourne University for example; perhaps I would have come across female mentors.

KEVIN: So do you mentor younger generation poets?

JENNIFER: I do, for that reason. I think it's really important. I feel strongly about that because I think I would have liked to find that myself.

* * *

KEVIN: How do you respond when you receive highly critical or negative responses to your work from the people who read it and comment on it?

JENNIFER: I accept that as being part of being a poet. I was going to say 'artist', but whether poet or artist you're actually inviting people to read your work and have opinions about it. Having another career can help buffer that because there's another area of self-esteem that isn't challenged. I wouldn't say that you are unaffected when somebody gets stuck into your work, but I don't feel it damages me or I necessarily have to engage with that person either.

KEVIN: Do you become more reluctant to show your work to that person?

JENNIFER: I probably wouldn't unless it was somebody I trusted.

KEVIN: Do you want to say anything about what kind of a role the publishing industry plays in your life as a writer? And including in that, writers' centres, festivals, etc.

JENNIFER: I've been lucky because I've had a publisher who has stuck with a small stable of writers and has affirmed their opinion of me as a writer over many books.

I have worked on books with other publishers as well. It's difficult for Australian poets to have the security of publishing but I haven't had that experience myself. Perhaps that's waiting for me, which might be good.

I have appeared at a few writers' festivals, reading poetry or participating in discussion. It's a danger to think that if you're not on a writing festival circuit you're a nobody. The bigger publishers have more money to promote certain authors. Often they're not poets, often they're nonfiction writers or novelists or high-profile politicians, for example. That can be damaging to poetry. There are very few poetry-only festivals, for example. Poets are out there, in that world. I find it disappointing at writers festivals when I don't see a good range of poets, local readings, discussion about poetry, poets on panels; poetry contributing a perspective to all sorts of issues. That is what I'd like to see more of.

* * *

KEVIN: There's this quote from Auden. *When we genuinely speak we do not have the words ready to do our bidding, we have to find them, and we do not know exactly what we are going to say until we've said it, and we say and hear something new that has never been said before or heard before.* I know this is putting you on the spot, but how do you respond to those few sentences and observations? What processes do you use to find the words to do your bidding?

JENNIFER: The things I relate to there are *genuinely speak*, and *something new that hasn't been said or heard before*.

To genuinely speak about poetry I need to discuss the fact that I had breast cancer repetitively for ten years from the age of 35; from when my son was one year old until he was 11. I had only resumed writing poetry shortly before that happened. The illness changed the perspective on everything in my life and poetry as well. My struggle to genuinely speak about that experience, without perhaps dealing overtly with content, has been one of the most important things I've dealt with in poetry. And also how to speak of cancer experience newly as it's never been spoken about before, because having a significant illness is not just my personal experience, it's a very common one.

Various modes of approach have been interesting to me. Even if I'm not wanting to write about it, it finds its way back into the lines, the imagery, emotional content, or an actual mention of something like a memory. It's like a nagging form that keeps coming in to the work and sometimes I wish it weren't there. I wish I could leave that behind and write without that knowledge that long illness brought. But you can't un-know it so it's become part of my writing.

Consciously, I've made other attempts to deal with it. The book, *Folly and Grief*,[7] which was about street performers and masks, and the long sequence 'Colombine' in *New and Selected Poems*,[8] were definite attempts to try and obtain some distance from myself and perhaps talk about it in different persona, with a mask. I don't know if that's answering Auden's question, but that's what it suggested to me.

KEVIN: It's as if the writing isn't quite under your control.

JENNIFER: Exactly. Yes. I don't think it ever is. I don't know if it is for others; certainly not really for me, and if I try too much it ruins the poetry actually.

KEVIN: Do you find material in conversation? And do you feel okay about taking things that friends and others might have said or told?

JENNIFER: I think I've only done it twice, with people I know. There was one poem about an incident when I was young and guests were coming for Christmas. My mother had Christmas presents but said, *let's only give it to them if they've got one for us*. And I put that in the poem. I wasn't game to show my mother that poem for many years. I did eventually 'fess up and she said, *well did you have to let all Australia know I said that?* She was quite a good sport about it.

KEVIN: Poetry has a very small audience though.

JENNIFER: That's right, I told her that.

KEVIN: You've said that German is a language other than English that's important in your practice. Does it go beyond German?

JENNIFER: Not really. I'm not particularly fluent in any other language. I've studied French and my daughter studied French to quite a high level. She's great to have as a resource when I need her advice.

I did live in New Guinea for six months, in Rabaul, in my young adult years. I've always loved the Pidgin language that we used living up there, something of a patois mix between Pidgin English and another whole sensibility of culture. I've put some inkling of that in a poem about Rabaul, about the earthquakes.[9] I put some Pidgin into that poem. Otherwise I don't practice translation.

KEVIN: Does music play a role in your practice?

JENNIFER: I wouldn't say it plays a large role in my practice of poetry. The musicality of poetry is quite different to other music. I don't play an instrument and I've often wondered how that would have changed one's listening to the lines or the rhythms of poetry. The rhythms in my poetry come from a different source from what we think of as traditional music. Perhaps the rhythm's more of childhood speech, for example.

KEVIN: That's interesting. So it's a more primitive music?

JENNIFER: It's an inner music or music that might not even be correct metrically at times, it's just some kind of rhythm in my ear for the way I hear words. It's probably an accretion of lots of different experiences, maybe some of those experiences of living overseas, the sound of UK English, the sound of American English. Eventually people began to think my accent was from South Africa, where I've never been. I like to listen to music, I love music, I love jazz and I love sitar and spent a long time travelling through India. I love Indian music and my husband and I love world music.

KEVIN: And do you have a critical voice that you apply to your composition as you're writing and can you identify where that comes from?

JENNIFER: I think the poets I've read and the mentors I've worked with and the conversations with many poets have all contributed to my personal internal editor. I write poetry on the run a bit too much. I would love the time to be more, as Seamus Heaney called it, *in the deep litter of the study*.[10] I don't often get a space of weeks to be in the deep litter of the study. I feel that as a lack, actually, the way my life is constructed as a mother, homemaker (sort of), psychiatrist and various other things in my life. I think in the deep litter of the study you probably can be immersed. The only book I felt I was like that in the writing was *Cudmirrah*, the *Cudmirrah* section of *Cabramatta/Cudmirrah*. I really enjoyed that experience of immersion.

KEVIN: How did you find the time then?

JENNIFER: As a younger person I could stay up most of the night, but I can't do that any more. I found the time, but it couldn't be sustained for a long time. I rarely practice like that now.

But in terms of the internal editor, I think I'm horribly harsh. I can be so horribly harsh on a poem that it disintegrates the poem. You know, sort of fiddling with it and still it's not quite right. The internal editor can be a noxious force. It's much better to work like a painter. They may do drawing sketches for a poem and they're not quite right, they have faults, but they are part of the process.

I might write the poem very quickly, but only after working through the failed sketches. I might do a first draft quickly and then, like a potter on a wheel, I thin it out. Then it collapses. I might go back to square one and thin it out a different way or shape it. Sometimes I'll go back to the original, write a new poem, and that's the poem.

KEVIN: Do you keep a record of those sketches, do you keep the documents?

JENNIFER: Oh, sometimes I find them so awful I throw them out.

KEVIN: And do you work on paper or do you work on the screen?

JENNIFER: I work on the computer, but I find you don't see faults in a poem necessarily, until you've printed it out.

KEVIN: Why do you think that is?

JENNIFER: The lines look different. You suddenly see the poem laid out on a page, you see it spatially. You mightn't be as happy with the line run-on, or where a line ending is, or the way it flows. It seemed all right on the screen but when you see it in a different modality it changes. That's the interaction between perception and text.

KEVIN: Do you have to be in the right mood to sit down and write, or does mood not have anything to do with it?

JENNIFER: I would like to be able to be dictated to by mood, but I can't. When I've got time I work on poems.

KEVIN: How differently do you experience creating and editing? Are they part of the same thing for you or are they two different processes?

JENNIFER: Completely different processes. I don't feel that the flow of inspiration, the spontaneous writing of a poem is the same process as an editing process. The editing process might release a new poem that's actually the poem you've been wanting.

KEVIN: So is the editing process less creative?

JENNIFER: I find it pernickety, and it's not my favourite part of poetry writing but it's necessary. In the creative flurry you might use several similar words in close proximity and their sameness detracts from the flow of the poem. Look at the rasa of the poem. It's the experience of the poem, how it feels, the rightness. If you have three words the same within two lines, unless intended, it detracts from the freshness. I see that as the editing process.

KEVIN: When you're writing, why do you stop writing? And connected with that, how do you finish poems?

JENNIFER: One is about completing a poem or knowing when to let it go, the other is about when to lay down the pen and have a break. I've never thought about this; I've thought about finishing poems but not when I take a break from a poetry session.

It can happen after one word, it can happen after several hours. It might be from frustration, might be you're not getting anywhere, it might be you're getting somewhere so you stay with it. It might be you've got pick up someone from cricket.

Finishing a poem is a different thing because a poem can take years to finish. It might be just the finishing that's the problem. There are some poems I've never finished and they're just waiting. Perhaps one day the finish will find me.

KEVIN: Do you go back to those poems regularly?

JENNIFER: I do, I revisit them.

KEVIN: Do you keep a folder or do you have them on your desktop?

JENNIFER: Electronically as well as hard copy. Not too many. Certain poems aren't finished because they're almost too private. I don't know that I'll ever show them or publish them. They might be about family or something like that; that's a different kind of finishing.

I feel that I never finish a book. Sometimes a poem will reappear in the next book, so it's a continual conversation. It's like, in psychoanalysis, the echoes of repetition, compulsions or words. I don't approach each book as something new. It's almost a continuation from the last one. That's a different way of not finishing.

KEVIN: And is there anything that readers owe you?

JENNIFER: Owe me? Just silence.

KEVIN: What about what you might owe readers? What obligations do you feel?

JENNIFER: Well I hate typos, and some of my books have typos. I really think you owe a reader not to have typos in the book.

KEVIN: So maybe what the readers owe you is to let you know when there are typos?

JENNIFER: Something like that.

NOTES

1   Kendall, Henry 1867 'Bell-birds', *The Sydney Morning Herald* no. 25 November

2   Jill Meagher, an Irish journalist working for the ABC and living in Melbourne, was raped and murdered in 2012 when walking home from a social engagement at night. Her attacker, Adrian Bayley, was sentenced to life imprisonment in 2013

3   Reg Grundy (1923-2016) was a pioneer of Australian media, particularly television, and a major contributor to popular culture in Australia

4   Harrison, Jennifer 1996 *Cabramatta/Cudmirrah*, Fitzroy North: Black Pepper

5   Tomas Tranströmer, 1931–2015; one of the major poets of his generation, he worked as a psychologist specialisng in disadvantaged groups, and was awarded the Nobel Prize in Literature in 2011

6   Marianne Moore met Elizabeth Bishop in 1934, when Bishop was in her final year of college, introduced by a librarian at the college. Their friendship—one of mentorship, creative generation, and mutual respect and affection—lasted until Moore's death in 1972. See Bishop's memoir-essay, 'Efforts of Affection: A Memoir of Marianne Moore' (in *Elizabeth Bishop: The Collected Prose*, ed. Robert Giroux, New York: Farrar, Straus and Giroux, 1984), on their relationship

7   Harrison, Jennifer 2006 *Folly and Grief,* Fitzroy North: Black Pepper

8   Harrison, Jennifer 2010 *Colombine: New and Selected poems,* Fitzroy North: Black Pepper

9   Harrison, Jennifer 1995 'Earthquake', in *Michelangelo's Prisoners*, North Fitzroy: Black Pepper Publishing

10 Seamus Heaney, '1973', from the long sonnet sequence Glanmore Revisited, published in *Seeing Things,* London: Faber & Faber, 1991

"Start up an idea, a poetry idea"
Jill Jones

University of Adelaide, Adelaide

JEN: What do you think about the points of connection you have to the world: what are they are to you and do they help you, or not, in your poetry?

JILL: First of all, I don't drive, I walk, or catch public transport, so I'm moving through the world in different ways to those usually in cars. Perhaps I see things slightly differently from some other people. I may not, of course.

JEN: It is different, though; you're at a slower pace.

JILL: Yes. And I've got to think about connections within cities and suburbs, and outside cities and suburbs. I've got to think about mapping in a slightly different way.

In another obvious way, I work with language, so my connection to the world is through written and spoken language. That's everywhere—signs, billboards, digital outlets, social media, talking or listening to people. I've also learnt from my students about how to talk about things in different ways, see language generationally.

JEN: A rubbing off of expertise in both ways?

JILL: Yes, exactly. I am often moved by what they say and write, and how they express their fears, their concerns, their experiences.

I'm always thinking about how language works and is manipulated. I've worked in a lot of bureaucracies, including university bureaucracies, where they fudge and mangle language. That's part of their business. I'm always reading something for both its surface and hidden structure. That's a big part of my connection. A kind of detective work.

I'm very connected to sound and vision. I've worked with creative artists in other areas, particularly visual artists. I love music. The rhythm of music means a lot to me, as well. It gets into many of my poems, a kind of beat or accent, though maybe only I can detect it specifically.

JEN: What is it that sustains you in your life, in your writing life?

JILL: Sometimes I think it's just my sheer stubbornness or bloody-mindedness. In the university you don't get sustained feedback about your creative research work. If somebody says something about it, that's helpful. It happens, though not that often. We're all preoccupied. And from readers or other writers, I get responses, here and there, sure, but . . . It's more that you just keep going. It sounds a bit terrible, doesn't it?

JEN: It sounds a bit like Beckett: *I can't go on, I'll go on.*[1]

JILL: Yes, I'll go on. I've had books published, that's something. I still get some poems accepted in journals, and that's also something. Apart from regular poetry reading series that most cities host, poets rarely get asked to do much publicly.

You just keep going, that's all you can do. Poetry isn't what you'd call a major or popular art form. So there must be some sort of strange compulsion to do it.

JEN: I do like your poetry very much, but to me it feels like there's a lot of existential doubt; or perhaps existential openness? I feel kind of a sadness running through a lot of your poems, and a slight wistfulness.

JILL: People have said that to me. For me, there's ever-present radical doubt about any number of things, so I would certainly say, *yes*. Whether that's a sad thing, maybe sometimes it is. One of my recent books is entitled *The Beautiful Anxiety*.[2] That title says a little of what I'm on about. People have said they think it's sad. I don't know that I felt sad when I was writing the poems in it. But doubt? Yes, absolutely. Doubt's not a bad thing. Unless you're a religious or political fundamentalist, presumably.

JEN: You've been writing poetry for a long time; do you remember where you first encountered poetry?

JILL: When I was a child. I remember, in primary school, we used to have these class readers and we'd be reading bush ballads and/or the great nineteenth-century looking-backwards tradition of English.

JEN: *Break, Break, Break on thy cold grey stones.*[3]

JILL: That sort of thing. I remember a teacher who used to get us to recite 'The Man from Snowy River' as a class.[4]

JEN: So you memorised poetry, too, at school?

JILL: 'Charge of the Light Brigade',[5] all of that kind of thing. I also came across some early twentieth-century stuff, a bit of DH Lawrence and such. By the time I'd got to first and second year at high school I was really interested in poetry.

I remember two particular poets who struck me at that age. One was Wordsworth, and his poem 'Upon Westminster Bridge'.[6] What that poem did for me as a kid was to say, you *can* write about cities. Poems don't always have to be about daffodils or Light Brigades or colts from Old Regret or knights and ladies of Shalott. You could just write about where you are, standing in the city.

The other poet we read a little bit later was Kenneth Slessor. He had a big influence on me at high school, especially *Five Bells*.[7] Also, how he wrote about the city and the country, such as in 'Country Towns',[8] and the poems he wrote about William Street.[9] All that was influential.

JEN: So, quite quotidian things, but rendered in a very imagistic way?

JILL: Yes, that's a good way to put it. I probably didn't realise at the time that Slessor was central to that flowering of modernism in Australian poetry. Still, I responded to his work very readily. A little later on I was exploring other ideas, poems and poetries—gracious, I discovered 'existentialism', as you do when you're 15—and I wrote some execrable verse. I've still got it somewhere and I'll have it destroyed if I know I'm about to die, but at the moment, I know it still exists and it keeps me honest. It took me a long time to get from writing that really bad stuff to where I am now. I was always scribbling something, but in my twenties I got distracted, so it took me a while to figure out that poetry was probably what I was still looking for.

JEN: Did you show people—friends or teachers—that 'execrable verse', when you were a teenager?

JILL: I might have shown a friend. Never a teacher. I certainly didn't show my parents. Not that there was anything disgraceful in it, but it was just strange, possibly embarrassing. One or two poems I might have later sent off to uni publications, when I was at university. They never saw the light of day. I said it was execrable.

I thought maybe I could write songs and I was hanging around people who played guitars but that didn't go anywhere.

JEN: So it had to be the poem rather than the song lyric?

JILL: Yes, because I wasn't terribly good at music. I could strum a guitar badly. That was about it. Also, I didn't want to write a song that someone else was going to sing and play around with, not at that stage in my life. Okay, it did happen just once. But nothing ever came of it.

JEN: Were you reading a lot of poetry at that age, apart from school-obligation reading?

JILL: I read for myself through my 20s, but in my 30s I really started to get back into it.

I met some people who were interested in the then modern American stuff, the political and feminist stuff. They were into Adrienne Rich, particularly *The Dream of a Common Language*.[10] From then on, I started to seek out more books and buy them and read them.

I didn't do English at university—oddly, if I think about it now—but I came across a lot of European poetry: Baudelaire, of course, and from the twentieth century, Montale, Tranströmer, Haavikko, and writers like that.[11] And there were those Penguin editions, where they'd include two or three poets in one slim volume. I still have a couple of those. I found Sylvia Plath, of course, but partly through an anthology I had bought edited by Al Alvarez, *The New Poetry*.[12] It included Peter Porter as well and Thom Gunn, Geoffrey Hill, Anne Sexton, John Berryman, and many more 1950s and 1960s poets. Well, a specific kind of 1950s and 1960s generation of poets. Because of the way that Australia was back then we were more exposed to British stuff than the Americans, or at least in my neck of the woods. The experience of other Australian poets and readers, I know in hindsight, was very different. While many had found the New York School poets, for instance, I took a while to get to all of that. I didn't hang around with a poetry crowd, I was never part of a scene.

JEN: So you're actually quite an isolated poet, then?

JILL: Back then, yes. I hung around people more interested in music, not poetry as such. Still, I kept it bubbling away and then, as I say, there was Adrienne Rich—very belatedly, this is Australia—and feminism, and a load of new stuff, to me, old stuff to others, I'm sure. What Rich was doing, particularly in her late 1960s and then 1970s poems, was clearly political but she also was writing about being a woman in the city, especially in the sequence 'Twenty One Love Poems'—it begins 'Whenever in this city, screens flicker . . .'[13]—and, for me, at a much later stage, that went *bing*! Of course, I could have been reading the New York poets and got something similar as well. But this was my particular experience of reading at a particular time. It was my 'coming out' time as well, so it makes sense.

JEN: So you dived into the wreck, too?[14] Was that where you started writing a lot?

JILL: Yes, absolutely. Part of this crowd of people I was hanging around with at that time were interested in 'the diary' again, it apparently was some kind of a 'thing', connected to 'creative liberation' if I recall correctly. So, I started to keep a diary, which I'd never done before. It's embarrassing stuff that I'd get rid of if I knew I was on death's door but I'm sure it still exists among my stuff. Anyway, all this writing turned towards poetry, not so much as confession but simply as putting my experience into language. I don't keep a diary now, I write poems, and I don't mean diary-like confessional poems. The diary idea lasted only over two or three years before this switch happened. And then I started to discover all the poetry that other people had discovered 10 years ago or 15 years before this. I don't read Rich all that much these days; not entirely sure why; but you have to acknowledge your sources.

* * *

JEN: In the here and now, if you meet a stranger and they ask you, *what do you do*, would you just say you're a poet; would you describe yourself in those ways?

JILL: It depends on the context. I may say that, but usually it's in the context that I teach at a university, that I teach creative writing. It's not because I don't want to say it, but sometimes people are really asking in a roundabout way where you work, which is an easier question to deal with.

JEN: Would you add a description to that? I'm a feminist poet? I'm a lyrical poet?

JILL: No. I wouldn't limit myself to a specific descriptor anyway. I don't think about my work like that. But I often get stumped, even annoyed when people ask 'and what sort of poetry do you write?'. Sometimes, I start to get explainy, give the potted version of the lecture

I gave the other day about . . . Which makes me feel like an uppity idiot very quickly. Or I might simply say, there are things that interest me, including writing about place and blah, blah, blah. That deflects some of it. It's odd that one can't simply say 'I write poetry'. The 'about' question always gets brought into the frame. I find that mystifying.

JEN: The 'writing about place' is a really interesting one. Do you find that your writing changes when you've changed your location; if you go overseas, if you move house?

JILL: That very idea has been on my mind ever since I moved from Sydney to Adelaide. It was obviously a big move and I think my writing has changed, mainly in its reference rather than the way I write. Nonetheless, I hope I'm doing different things, staying fresh. Doing different things with the words so that the poetry as a structure will change. But certainly, there's a lot more desert and dry air in the poems, more plains instead of valleys.

JEN: So you're not an Adelaide poet nor a Sydney poet?

JILL: No, I'm not either. I don't live in Sydney so I'm no longer a Sydney poet, although, some people still think I live there even after all these years. And plenty of newer poets in Sydney now would never have even met me, understandably. And Adelaide . . . let's just say, I suspect I'm still regarded by many as a newcomer, or a Sydney poet in disguise.

JEN: Do you have relationships with other poets?

JILL: Here in Adelaide I go to a lot of readings and events where I catch up with people and I've made friendships through that. One happy result of that is that a couple of years back poet Alison Flett and I started discussing the idea of a small chapbook series, that we ended up calling Little Windows. We launched the first series of chapbooks in 2016 and did a second in 2017. Our idea is to publish four poets a time, at least one of whom is South Australian—so far, they've been us two, plus Ali Cobby Eckermann and Kathryn Hummel; and another one or two are non-SA Australians: so far, Andy Jackson and Adam Aitken—and one who is not Australian. Given Alison's Scots background, these latter non-Australians have been Scottish or Scots-based, at least so far—John Glenday and Jen Hadfield. So, the local and the international or, as our wee website has it, 'little books, big horizons'.[15]

Of course, I teach and have taught poets who live here, or who lived here and have now left, that Adelaide exodus thing. Some of them stay in touch after they graduate, or I knew them before they began studying with me. All that's slightly complicated sometimes.

People say to me, or I hear through the grapevine which is easy to do in Adelaide, that my poetry is thought to be a bit 'difficult', for some reason I can't quite figure out. Because it really isn't difficult. So, yes, I take part in a fair bit of what goes on but I've learnt to ponder some things more quietly.

*　　*　　*

JEN: Is there anyone who reads your early drafts? Do you have a relationship of exchange with another poet or someone you trust?

JILL: I feel everyone's so busy these days that I'm always reluctant to ask. Also, as I've been, or still am, a supervisor of some of poets' work here, it can be a tricky thing to negotiate. I get that. My partner has looked at my poems over many years and gives me good advice. Here in Adelaide, I've one very good friend, a poet, who kindly looks at manuscripts and poems from time to time, and I return the favour. Depending on the circumstance, she has given me feedback on individual poems but, especially, has given me some crucial and canny feedback on a manuscript.

JEN: The flow of poems, the structure of it?

JILL: Yes, that sort of thing. Very important.

Many years ago, in Sydney, I used to go to one or other poetry or writing group where we'd talk about our work, and I do recall the specific kind of camaraderie and engagement that produced. Different places, different times!

JEN: Are there any effects that you'd like to have on your readers, whether it's a reader of a reasonably early draft or if it's a finished work?

JILL: I'd certainly be happy if people got some pleasure out of what I write. But first up, I would simply like people to read my work and get something from it, in whatever way works for them. I'm not trying to be understood in the sense that you could write it out in bullet points.

JEN: You could explain it in an essay if you could explain that way.

JILL: Yes, exactly. You might as well write the essay and actually enjoy doing that. There's always some enjoyment in any writing, in the play of language, and maybe a hybrid poem-essay would be a something I could do, in fact I have done it, years ago.[16] Of course, that's not what you mean. Besides, I'm not trying to foment revolution.

JEN: Oh, come on, let's do it!

JILL: I think we might have to. Or make a point, although there are times when I'm trying to make more of a point than just play with language.

JEN: I haven't found a didactic register in your poetry.

JILL: That's good to know. If ever I find myself sliding into that register, I pull back. I like to play, in that broad sense, rather than preach. I like to think that people can go along with the play, if that's an effect?

JEN: We can call that an effect; it's a way of connecting, a way of engaging. And the creative activity, I think, makes you think in a particular way.

JILL: Sometimes, I'm sitting up late at night, just talking to myself, not in a weird way or an aloud way but trying things out. Along with that can come autobiographical detail or biographical detail, or memory, even though I might put a slant on it, which I know is not me.

JEN: It might be what's actually happening in a part of your life and then you mediate it and modulate it?

JILL: For me, it's not completely dissimilar to the sorts of things Ken Bolton or Pam Brown might do. Not the same, of course, but not all that far distant from it, that idea of writing the contemporary moment. It's one side of some things I've been doing.

*   *   *

JEN: Moving along to questions of practice, I sent you that Auden quote: *when we genuinely speak, we do not have the words ready to do our bidding; we have to find them. We don't know exactly what we're going to say until we've said it. And then we say and hear something new, it's never been said or heard before.* And we're asking all the poets this because it's in one way, very obvious; but in other way, it can lead to all kinds of thoughts about what those words are, do they do our bidding, can they do our bidding?

JILL: It raises a whole issue around one's poetics. If you set up constraints, have you already told the words to do certain prescribed things or does something happen between?

In what I try to do, I'm hoping my current writing is not the same as I've always done. I don't believe in the adage that you always end up writing the same poem, but I worry that it might happen too often.

I've got two sides to what I do. One is, for want of a better word, conceptual where I do set up something as a concept or constraint, but I usually muddy those waters. A pure conceptual poet wouldn't do that, the seventh noun along in the dictionary is what goes into the poem instead of this noun 'daffodil', no matter what.

JEN: Because the 'rule' says so?

JILL: 'Because the rule says so and I'm not changing it.' And that's fine. Sometimes I go in that direction. But I've always had problems with purity.

On the other hand, I hear something, I see something, I think about something, on the news or out in the world, and I will, in my own way, write something about it or out of it and start up an idea, a poetry idea, not an intellectual idea, and see where that leads. I'll think about the sounds of the language I'm using and I might think: will I repeat these phrases? Will I look at some of the sound effects that might be going on here? Or the rhythmic effects of the line? Or will I just write down what I'm hearing at the moment and see what happens?. It becomes a list of approaches. And could be partly to do with what I'm experiencing at the time: have I been out talking to people? Or do I have a cold? Am I tired?

JEN: Do you also take material you find in overheard speech, conversations, other people's experiences?

JILL: Oh, yes. I lift the overheard from everywhere; travelling on public transport you hear so many things. Plus, we're bombarded with phrases every day. You sometimes write down advertising copy and mangle it, add a political spin. Same with song lyrics, or a turn of phrase that someone might use.

JEN: And steal it, unashamedly?

JILL: Yes, and then work it. Of course, as you know, you always need to be careful if you're quoting from another piece of text. It can get complicated and trips people up. Even if you hope you remember where you got it from, sometimes you do forget where, it does happen. You need to find out if it is in the public domain or copyright. Sometimes you assume that people have read all the things that you've read and, therefore, they will know that you're referring to a phrase by TS Eliot or Gwen Harwood or someone else, and they don't, and therefore they think you've stolen something. And you think, *but surely everyone knew that*. I know there's stuff in my work that's a bit like that. In a broad sense, we are thieves, that's what we do, using the language that exists and texts that are part of our lives.

I wrote a poem I included in *The Beautiful Anxiety*[17] that consisted solely of phrases or parts of phrases from other poems that began with *I*. A cento, if you will. It was a poem about the I in the poem and it was partly ironic, partly fun and partly, well, what does *I* mean in the poem? What is subjectivity? Granted, some of the phrases you almost wouldn't recognise unless I told you which poem they came from. Some of them I thought were blindingly obvious because they were from classic poems. But in the interests of acknowledging my sources, I had to go through every phrase and footnote it . . . this comes from Rochester, this from Shakespeare, this from Robert Lowell, Marianne Moore, and, and, and, and. Just to cover my butt.

JEN: TS Eliot heavily annotated and footnoted a lot of his poems. It's a perfectly valid approach to take.

JILL: Of course it is. I put the footnotes into the acknowledgements page of the book. It's only a short poem, so they were longer than the poem.

JEN: How about languages other than English? You've read the nine-teenth-century French poets—in translation, presumably? Do you have other languages?

JILL: Not enough to do more than order a glass of wine in a café in Paris. Well, I can do a little more than that with my bad French but not terribly much more. Same with my school-girl German.

However, I have actually done my own translations of various poems. I rely, first of all, on transliterations and if I can get more than one of those, that's good. Then I consult other translations, as opposed to absolute transliterations, and I do some research around the original poem if possible. Then I work up my own version. I've published one or two of these, and people native or well-versed in the original lan-guages have been kind about my 'translation'. It's a useful exercise to do just for yourself, to be both thinking about the original poem as well as the process of translation.

JEN: What about other people's critical voices? They might be dead people, live people, people you know, or people in books: do you rely on any of those when you're actually making or editing your work?

JILL: I suppose, yes, in the sense that the tradition's always there in front of you rather than behind you. You are usually aware of what people have said about x or y's poems and how they work, so you might decide to write 'near' them. But what does it really mean to begin writing a poem after reading someone else's; to be writing, say, after reading O'Hara or Niedecker, Stein or Prynne? You're not just using it as a simple jumping off point, because you're already in amongst a complex of types or forms of writing, critique, opinion, 'schools'. For instance, I sit here and, see those shelves, there's all these books of poetry, fiction, and critical writing. It's all in front of me.

JEN: Both physically and metaphorically, it's right there?

JILL: It's there. It's not as though you're leaving it behind. It just gets added to and changed. You change your mind about it, continually. Well, I do.

JEN: You mentioned reading somebody else and maybe thinking about writing along those lines, and the next question is about the process of composition: do you find you have to be in the right mood to compose? Is there any mood involved, for you, in composition?

JILL: There must be a mood. But I'm not sure what it is because I've written when tranquil and I've written when frustrated, I've written when tired and I've written when relaxed. It's not really those kinds of states, for me. It also depends on what kind of poem I might start to write. So, maybe it's to do with atmosphere. If late at night, after I've had conversation and a glass of wine with a meal, I'll sit down and write in a certain way. If I'm sitting on a bus heading to wherever, just scribbling, I'll be writing in a different way or mood.

JEN: You don't seek out the mood, you allow it to inform your practice at that moment?

JILL: It's a bit of both. In semester time, if I'm going to write, I have to squeeze it in somewhere between teaching, supervising, marking, doing all the admin. I try to write most days but it often doesn't work. For instance, I was writing at least a couple of lines, even if they were crap lines, up until about this week, and then it just hasn't happened.

My writing, I'm finding at the moment, is fragmentary. If I'm writing in a certain way, a style, let's say, it makes me wonder, could this be the basis of something that I should continue to do? That I use, in a sense, where I am with the writing to guide further writing. If you can't find the space, make the space you have work for you.

JEN: Yes, so if you've got fragments, you work with fragments?

JILL: That's what I mean, yes. Even bits and pieces I post on social media can be worked into that idea. But next year I may not be writing in fragments. I might be making lists. I might be writing dialogues. I might be doing prose poems. Who knows?

It's making use of what you've got. I think of poetry as the art of making something. It's crafting, or a makingness, and you're making it out of materials, language, the place you are, the time you have, the body you have.

You're putting those materials somewhere, whether you're scribbling on a piece of paper or you're putting it on a screen, painting it on a wall or writing on a whiteboard. Putting it into little secret envelopes and sealing them up. Anything. And the materials you use, the actual literal materials, contribute to what you're doing.

JEN: Do you write quickly? Can you get a first draft out quite quickly or are you a slower producer?

JILL: Mostly, I write quickly, once I get going, though that's not always the case. People have called me 'prolific' in an almost accusatory sense, which is odd in itself, but I'm no more prolific than a number of other poets I could name (but won't). And I've had my not so prolific times as well. So, I write a lot of drafts, notes, but there's a lot which is unpublishable, that goes without saying. Or it may take time to get it to publishable stage. I've got drafts that I've produced quickly which then have been sitting around for a decade or longer, in a notebook, a file, on an envelope even.

JEN: A long slow cellaring process, in some cases?

JILL: Yes, precisely. Sometimes the difference between the first draft and the final draft is quite minimal, but mostly the changes are substantial. Plenty of poems I've written, I've realised were failures as a whole, so I've picked them apart and combined them with other material to make a completely new poem. Sometimes that will take days, weeks, months or years.

JEN: Are composing and editing the same process for you, or are they are different when you do them?

JILL: Editing's probably a different mindset. Though there's always going to be a bit of self-editing along the way, as you write a line and think, oh, no, that sounds awkward, I'll write this instead. Lots of crossing out in the writing process.

JEN: How do you know when a poem is done?

JILL: I don't think you do. Or I don't think I do. Some poems I do, of course. Sometimes I just get tired of a poem and I either put it out there or put it away. In other words, it works or it doesn't work. At least on some external criteria.

JEN: Or it goes in the drawer?

JILL: Or it goes in the drawer and then ten years later, I bring it out, and think, oh, that's actually alright. Also, editorial and reader interests change and what you couldn't place anywhere ten years ago can find publication today or soon.

JEN: Where there is emotion in your practice is it about you or is it about the thing that's happening in the poem? Is it something, in other words, are you driven there by emotion or is the effect of the poem to generate emotion of somebody else or to kind of manifest an emotional state in a poetic persona?

JILL: That's a very interesting question. It varies. Poems come out of states of being and action, even conceptual work comes out of that. It's possibly a mixture of both, if that's not fudging the answer. I've learnt not to expect a specific reaction from people about a poem. Something I think is funny, they don't, and vice versa. I'm often surprised when people say *Oh, you seem very sad.* And I think, I'm not sad at all. I may be quiet, but that's a different thing. And what has that got to do with the poem?

JEN: *Not sad at all,* in which case we might be reflecting our own sadness in reading those lines.

JILL: It may have something to do with perplexity, it might be anger.

JEN: Some people register their own anger as sadness. A lot of depression is actually rage.

JILL: Yes, exactly, yes. In an issue of *Jacket2* a while ago,[19] Michael Farrell picked up on a couple of poems of mine, one in *Dark Bright Doors* called 'Leaving it to the Sky',[20] and another one called 'Misinterpretations/or the Dark Grey Outline', that was first published in *Overland*,[21] and then included in *The Beautiful Anxiety*. He noted, positively, that I was sounding more impatient, more assertive, and I think he really got that affective register.

JEN: With the impatient poems, when he said that, did you say *yes, I always knew that*, to yourself or did you think, *oh, yeah, that's right*?

JILL: I'd written poems like that before, at least I felt I had, but maybe it came through more clearly in these. And that's that whole problem of what you think you're doing and what people think you're doing, and whether there's this third sort of mysterious entity which is what the poem actually is. No, that's making it sound much too mysterious or metaphysical. But maybe there is a third position between what you think you're doing, what people think it is, and the thing that exists as is (the poem, let's say). Especially when that poem thing appears to others to be significantly different to what you thought you were writing. Because we all have our own relationship with language, and it's always changing. Language will do various things to various people at various times. I don't govern the language even as I write a poem.

JEN: The language governs itself but the poet whittles it into shape and then the reader reads it in a shape.

JILL: Given that language is a human construct, it's not something that lives by itself. It's as though we've created this virtual entity called language and it has a certain life or way of working for the poet, the reader.

JEN: Yes, it's such a tricky thing. Clearly, language does construct us but as you say, we actually make it up and continue to make it up every day. But there's things we can only do because language allows us to.

JILL: Yes, as a poet, I see I've made something out of language, but what does another reader make of what I've made? I can't make too many assumptions about that process, of reading. And, let's not forget that poets are also readers (one hopes). Of course, I can probably assume that, because I've been asked to read poems to an audience, or readers have bought my book, then they have some interest in it. That's about as far as I can go. Some people, from time to time, will say kind, meaningful, insightful and helpful things. Or unkind or negative things. Yes, that's about as far as it goes.

JEN: That's pretty fine.

The last question is throwing a mouse into the middle of the room. It's is there anything your readers owe you?

JILL: If they stole a book of mine they'd probably owe someone some money. Maybe me, or a bookseller.

No, seriously, I've never thought of readers owing writers anything. Are we even to be respected? I don't think we're necessarily respectable people. You would like to think that some readers may offer up a response, but they don't owe me that. I often prefer to keep my opinion about my reading of certain texts to myself.

I would like to think, at a very basic level, if I got up to read poems, that the audience would at least keep quiet and listen. There's no owing there, it's simply respecting the occasion, which doesn't simply revolve around the poet. I can't imagine why any poet would think they're owed something, but possibly some do.

JEN: I have to say of the poets we've interviewed so far nobody really thinks anybody owes them anything except, as you say, *if you're reading, read it*, and *if you're listening, be quiet while I'm speaking*. That's about it.

I'm getting more interested in this as it goes along. It seems to me that what poets are saying is that poetry really is different from the other 'creative' industries. We know we're not going to get money and so we don't expect that; we know we're going to get little, if any, praise, so we don't expect that. With the other creative things we do, we do expect something back; we do feel owed in some way, it seems; but poetry does seem to sit off to the side.

JILL: Yes; which, to use that terrible phrase, is both its strength and its weakness. And, though poetry sits to the side from a career or money-making sense, it's also at the heart of things because it's noncompliant. Plato wanted to kick us out of the republic, and plenty of other people have wanted to do the equivalent of that and have, in fact, done it since forever. Poets have been killed, are being killed, for their writing, as we know.

JEN: Maybe because it is non-propositional and isn't easily controlled.

JILL: It's working at the heart of language. Poetry is always challenging how language works, including all that controlling.

NOTES

1   Beckett, Samuel 1977 [1953] 'The Unnameable', in *The Trilogy*, London: Everyman's Library

2   Jones, Jill 2013 *The Beautiful Anxiety*, Glebe: Puncher and Wattmann

3   Tennyson, Lord Alfred 1842 'Break, Break, Break', in *Poems*, London: Edward Moxon, 287

4   Paterson, AB 1895 'The Man from Snowy River', in *The Man from Snowy River and Other Verses*, London: Angus and Robertson, 5–8

5   Tennyson, Lord Alfred 1854 'Charge of the Light Brigade', *The Examiner*, 9 December

6   Wordsworth, William 1807 'Composed upon Westminster Bridge, September 3, 1802', in *Poems in Two Volumes*, London: Longman, 118–120

7   Slessor, Kenneth 1939 'Five Bells', in *Five Bells: XX Poems*, Sydney: Frank Johnson, 15–20

8   Slessor, Kenneth 1944 'Country Towns', in *One Hundred Poems: 1919-1939*, Sydney: Angus and Robertson, 81

9   Slessor, Kenneth 1939 'William Street', in *Five Bells: XX Poems*, Sydney: Frank Johnson, 33

10 Rich, Adrienne 1978 *The Dream of a Common Language. Poems, 1974-1977* New York: Norton

11 Charles Baudelaire (1821–1867), an important early writer of prose poetry, but perhaps best known for his collection *Les Fleurs du mal* (1857); Italian poet Eugenio Montale (1896–1981) was awarded the Nobel Prize in Literature for 1975; Tomas Tranströmer (1931–2015), poet and psychologist, won the Nobel in 2011; Finnish poet Paavo Haavikko (1931–2008) won the Neustadt International Prize for Literature in 1984

12 Alvarez, Al 1962 *The New Poetry: An Anthology*, London: Penguin

13 Rich, Adrienne 1978 *The Dream of a Common Language. Poems, 1974-1977*, New York: Norton

14 'Diving into the wreck' is one of Adrienne Rich's widely anthologised poems, and also the title of her 1973 collection, *Poems 1971–1972*, New York: WW Norton

15 See https://littlewindowspress.com/

16 See Jill Jones 2003 'What is the electric life of words?', *Southern Review* 36.3

17 Jones, Jill 2013 *The Beautiful Anxiety*, Glebe: Puncher and Wattmann

18 Frank O'Hara (1926–1966) was a prominent member of the New York School poets; Lorine Niedecker (1903–1970), an Objectivist poet, wrote

imagistic poems often reflecting on nature; Gertrude Stein (1874–1946), a modernist and highly experimental writer; JH Prynne, British poet and academic

19 Farrell, Michael 2011 'Magazines #8 overland 204', *Jacket2* https://jacket2. org/commentary/magazines-8

20 Jones, Jill 2010 *Dark Bright Doors,* Kent Town: Wakefield Press

21 Jones, Jill 2011 'Misinterpretations / or the Dark Grey Outline', *Overland* 204 Spring 2011, https://overland.org.au/previous-issues/issue-204/ poem-jill-jones/

"Genuinely speaking"
Justin Clemens

Melbourne, Victoria

KEVIN: Justin, thanks for agreeing to do this.

JUSTIN: A pleasure, Kevin.

KEVIN: We're going to start with the question of conditions and contexts. We start from the assumption that any poet is connected to the world through their poetry. How do you see your points of connection to the world through your poetry?

JUSTIN: Mm, it's a hard question. I'm more connected to the world through poetry than the other way around. I *read* poetry *to* think about the world rather than the world to think about poetry. John Forbes used to say poetry just gets you there faster. So I think poetry *is* the world, the world appears through poetry and that's the way of encountering it.

KEVIN: Is poetry reading, then, central to your work?

JUSTIN: Yes, poetry reading is absolutely central to my work.

KEVIN: And where does poetry writing sit in relation to your work?

JUSTIN: You mean my writing, in particular? I don't have enough time to do it. I would like to do more of it because you can't write unless you read. Otherwise it doesn't make any sense. Melbourne is full of exciting poets all pumping stuff out. You see them at readings and launches and online stuff and magazines and so on. I'd just like more time to write, really.

KEVIN: So, given the struggle you have to find time to write, what has kept you writing through your life thus far?

JUSTIN: In terms of the sort of work that I do, I would like it to be better. It's not as good as I would like it to be. There are modes which affect the form of my work. I remember, years ago, Tony Birch saying he was writing short poems because he had 200 kids.[1] The only time he could get to write anything at all was between the time they'd fallen asleep and before he'd fallen asleep. So he was writing tiny little memory lyrics. They were fantastic, but you could see that the time he had affected the form of his work. Now, he's a short story writer. I did something a bit different with *The Mundiad*,[2] which I've been writing since the late 1990s; it is a long poem in rhyming couplets. My plan is to iterate it, and iterate it in more and more books as a life project. You can write a rhyming couplet relatively quickly, then it becomes aggregative. That's affected, and is effective, for my work. Rather than writing punctual little lyrics most of the time, I'm writing couplets. Couplets are a bit cheap now as a form, but they're ancient, really.

The attentiveness one has to bring to bear to read them is a totally different one from radical contemporary experimental poetry which requires different sorts of both reading and writing attention. The form of my work, in so far as it's been linked for a long time to this ongoing volume, has enabled me to keep writing. Writing for a long time, writing and perfecting a form, but that form being tied to having to steal time. The length, the gigantism of it, is linked to a lack of time rather than a lot of free time.

KEVIN: That's interesting, isn't it? Someone like William Carlos Williams could root his minimalism in his busy life as a doctor and lack of time to write. But then someone like William Blake, who also worked in the rhyming couplet, had endless time but he reverted to a similar method to what you've got, despite him having all that time.

JUSTIN: That's right. I don't think you can read the form and the life off in a one-to-one correspondence. To come back to what you were saying about creativity, part of the problematic of creativity is creating. You're creating a form, or recreating an existing form, that's going to work for you, but doesn't necessarily have a one-to-one correspondence. So, I have no time but that doesn't mean I write tiny short poems like WCW or Tony Birch. I've almost no time, so the poem becomes very, very, very, very long but it takes on this little couplet clutch, clutch, clutch, clutch. They're little pincers of time.

*   *   *

KEVIN: Can you remember your first encounter with poetry?

JUSTIN: There's two things I remember specifically about poetry as a child; I was about seven in both cases. The first one was reading, *Jabberwocky* by Lewis Carroll.[3] I just thought it was the best thing ever so I memorised it straight away. I thought it was fucking great and that was the only way to have it permanently.

About the same time there was an anthology of American poetry from the late seventeenth century to the mid-1960s. It had a selection of small people. (Auden was counted as an American poet.) I just read it through. It had all these people we've not heard of. I loved that little book.

KEVIN: And was it your parents who exposed you to that?

JUSTIN: I don't know where the book came from; I literally don't. I just ended up with this book and I just don't know where it came from. From a junk store, or maybe my parents gave it to me, or maybe it was lying around. I acquired it somehow. I remember reading and reading this book. It literally fell apart after thirty-five years of reading and it was already old when I'd got it.

KEVIN: You're still reading poetry a lot?

JUSTIN: I read a lot of poetry. Contemporary poetry's different from the modern poetry, obviously. I was reading modern poetry as a child and now I'm reading contemporary. I'm not sure I like contemporary that much and I'm not sure I understand it all the time. But it is poetry and it is contemporary so I feel I should keep reading it.

KEVIN: Do you describe yourself as a poet when you are introduced, or introduce yourself, to people?

JUSTIN: No, I feel a bit embarrassed about it, really. I don't mind other people saying it but I prefer not to be there when they do.

KEVIN: Why is that?

JUSTIN: Mainly because of an infantile fantasy that being a poet is not for you to say. It's honorific, right? Lots of people write poetry, it doesn't make them fucking poets. I find it a bit embarrassing.

KEVIN: You're not unusual. About ninety per cent of the answers we get are along those lines.

JUSTIN: That's great. Sorry. That's reassuring, right?

KEVIN: The title of poet has a curious cultural societal resonance not many people want to enter into, explicitly anyway. So if people do recognise you as a poet the next question always is, what kind of poetry? What kind of poet are you?

JUSTIN: The name *poet* has lots of problems. One of them is that it presumes you're a good poet. It presumes you have to have done something good or specific. This is linked to timing, the time of poetry. A poet is dated and non-dated at the same time. I have *The Mundiad* which looks very ancient but it's in the form. Is it possible to write poetry—not just verse but poetry—in a contemporary form, in an old form?

But then, I've been writing lots of weird homophonic work. The latest two things I've got published are in *Bumf,* which is an online Queensland magazine. They commissioned something around the

G20.[4] I wrote a homophonic poem based on Australian governmental crap about the G80 which is the G20. It takes original text of the government and exposes it for the gibberish that it is, in a slightly hilarious way. I see that as a contemporary post-formal mode of working. The other thing is palindrome; writing massively long palindromes, with all of the pointlessness, but it's full-on.

KEVIN: You've got a dictionary of palindromes, or you're searching for them?

JUSTIN: Oh no, no, no. That's the thing; the pointlessness about palindromes these days is with computerisation: you press the button and the computer generates it. I want to generate a perfectly nonsensical computer palindrome, but by working it out every step of the way myself. So it's not the product, it's the process that's gone into it. This pointless, repetitive, nonsensical enterprise that's integrated: that's the point of it, really; and that's poetry.

KEVIN: Have you got the word radar in there?

JUSTIN: Yeah, radar turns up every now and again. There's a whole load. *Able Was I Ere I Saw Elba*, which is the choice one about Napoleon.

KEVIN: Great. The next question was, how might you engage with social issues in your poetry?

JUSTIN: The issue of labour for me, at the moment, is in these palindromes and post-formal experimentation. It's about forms of immaterial labour which can be done just as well by an algorithm; in fact, better with an algorithm.

KEVIN: And what about location, home and movement. Does your writing change according to where you live or your shifts in living locations? Is home important to you?

JUSTIN: I love Melbourne. There's George Steiner's thing about *my homeland is my typewriter*.[5] Back to your first question, the world is opened through poetry; you don't go from the world into poetry. It's important to invert the order. If there's a home, it's the two things that I really care about. One of them is poetry and the other one is philosophy.

KEVIN: How different do you see those two realms?

JUSTIN: I see them as imbricated antitheses. You can't have one without the other and they are very old. As Plato says in *The Republic*, a very old antagonism is like an old war, and it's an essential war.

KEVIN: So did you go from poetry to philosophy?

JUSTIN: It's poetry that's first, it must be first. Poetry is the ground of everything that it doesn't say. Philosophy says poetry lies so you can only open the world with poetry but you can't run the world with poetry, or you can't run a just world. That's a basic relation, isn't it? Poetry opens a world but then you can't run it with poetry.

KEVIN: That's a good way of putting it; which brings us to the question of your education. How has education shaped the poetry you write?

JUSTIN: My father was in the British Army. I was born in Hong Kong and I grew up on Malta and Cyprus. I grew up on British Army bases until we came to Melbourne when I was just about to be a teenager. My education's been a weird military school education.

KEVIN: On the assumption you were going to join the military?

JUSTIN: No, no, no, just because you have to dump your kids somewhere when you've got the fathers on base. They're really fantastic places, army bases.

It was a weird time for the British Army. They weren't in any conflict so it was full of English guys having a permanent paid holiday. Drinking in other people's countries. It was pretty odd.

But education: the syllabus at those schools was about doing an O level or an A level in the English system, eventually. It had no military direction, specifically, although the games you play after school are war games. The schools would finish early, particularly in Cyprus, because the British thought it was too hot after lunchtime to do anything in the afternoon. School started at 7:30 in the morning, and finished at 1:15. The whole afternoon we'd either swim or play war.

I don't have a lot of the problems with the military or war or warfare that lots of people seem to have. But also I'm not saying war's good or the military's good. It was a revolting colonial enterprise in which it was involved. But there's some other things about it that are quite good. That education had poetry in the English syllabus as an integral part of the English primary and secondary syllabus.

KEVIN: Probably more poetry than an Australian education would have had?

JUSTIN: Probably, because it's also linked to the nationalism of the British Empire; we have great poets.

KEVIN: Claiming the Irish poets, too?

JUSTIN: Yeah, of course and the Scots. And the Welsh and the . . . exactly.

KEVIN: How did you move from that education to university; and did poetry follow you through into that transition?

JUSTIN: I was quite lucky in a weird unlucky way. I did my university degree here, I started in 1987. The English department here was massive and still completely divided. From my perspective, it was divided between the new school theory guys, like David Bennett, and the old school guys who'd be someone like Vin Buckley or Peter Steele or Chris Wallace-Crabbe.

So there's all these guys who were interested in a kind of idea of poetry, and then there was the new studies; you know, you read the theory rather than the thing itself. And so the old guys seemed old and not very hip. That's a problem. I did a couple of Vin Buckley's courses and they were fantastic, just in terms of bringing people to sing out some ballad, like old border ballads as part of the class. He had some amazing readings of Yeats, those sorts of things. That poetry was still integral even if it came across as a bit old hat or not very hip.

And then the new stuff was the only way that philosophy continued, bizarrely, in Australian universities. The philosophy department here was an abomination and a travesty. So was the theory, but at least it permitted the harbouring of an institution that was germane to both poetry and philosophy. It was both good and bad, Kevin.

KEVIN: And your relationships to other poets: how does that work with your poetry?

JUSTIN: I'm quite solitary as a poet, as an actual writer of poetry. One of the things I've noticed about a lot of the younger poets is they're in little groupuscles of self-organising, self-forming, almost militarised warfare. While I hang out with some of those people, I don't often see myself as participating, specifically, in their group.

KEVIN: I think the discovery of a community, if you're lucky, is the thing that happens in your twenties. And it's exciting.

JUSTIN: Absolutely. And I never had that as a poet. Also, I think it is always ambivalent. I don't remember it really being around in that way. I see that as the end of the old university. That's another sequence that ended around 1990 with the restructuring of the relationship between economy and the society in Australia. And of the beginnings of the reign of the internet. It was the end of a sequence, for universities and university education; everything was different, people didn't necessarily need to feel the *penguin clustering* in groups.

KEVIN: And so now, are there others that you show your drafts to?

JUSTIN: No. Things would benefit from that, I'm sure my drafts would benefit. I'd show my publisher, at the moment, John Hunter, who's doing a lot of poetry publishing. He's a great reader but he doesn't have the same intensity that a poet would.

KEVIN: Has there been, in the past, anyone who's read your work?

JUSTIN: No, I feel that's a loss. but that's been part of my . . . *he never was a joiner*, as John Forbes says.[6] Towards the end of his life John Forbes would give me drafts of his poems. I don't know if he wanted my feedback, or if it would have been any use to him. He would, at least, distribute the poems. I won't even normally do that.

KEVIN: I'll ask you more about your process in a minute but before we move onto that, are there any particular effects you want to have on your readers?

JUSTIN: Yeah. I want people to go: *that's fucking amazing*; that's all. I don't think they have to feel happy, sad, moved, excited, anxious. Poetry can produce and harbour all affects and all responses. You need good readers, you don't just need writers; that's part of the problem. Even if they're the same people, there should be a stringent division between them which maybe comes back to my lack of joining.

KEVIN: A stringent division between . . . ?

JUSTIN: Between being a reader and a writer. Even if they're exactly the same person and exactly the same thing, you need to go beyond the sphere of reciprocity in writing and reading. They're both absolutely vital, and good readers are at least as important as good writers.

KEVIN: So is Justin the reader a different person from Justin the writer?

JUSTIN: Yes, yes, absolutely.

KEVIN: And does the reader have a role to play in the process of writing?

JUSTIN: Yes, absolutely.

KEVIN: . . . I mean Justin the reader?

JUSTIN: Yes, absolutely. They're still, once again, an imbricated antithesis. That's a principle I would fervently maintain. The identity is that of discontinuity.

KEVIN: With this question of creativity you'd have to argue that the writer brings a certain kind of creativity to the task, and the reader also brings their own creativity to the task.

JUSTIN: They do. Absolutely. To be honest, I'm a much better reader than I am a writer. My reading is evident in some of my writing but not necessarily. It's all creative, but it's not necessarily poetry, to come back to the specifically honorific and elevated place I clearly assign to that.

*   *   *

KEVIN: We've got a quote here that I'm sure you looked at when you were looking at the questions, Auden's quote. Do you want me to read it to you?

JUSTIN: Please do.

KEVIN: *When we genuinely speak, we don't have the words ready to do our bidding; we have to find them and we don't know exactly what we're going to say until we've said it and we say and hear something new that's never been said or heard before.* Do you have a response to that? And connected with that question, what processes do you use to find the words to do your bidding?

JUSTIN: I really love Auden as a writer. There's a couple of things here. One are things that Auden says, which are poetic process. And one is that you stop being a poet as soon as you put down your pen or whatever, right?

KEVIN: Yes.

JUSTIN: So poetry is the act of writing, but also the act of writing is not having words ready. It's actually a process which is constantly interrupted by its own incapacity.

Auden's one of those geniuses who can phrase things so simply when he talks in this metapoetic sense, and yet they're super profound. So the emphasis must be on genuine speaking or, as he defines poetry elsewhere, poetry's *memorable speech*.[7] Other people want to remember it, right? It's genuinely speaking; it's a voice you haven't heard before.

I think of Les Murray as genuinely a voice, he genuinely speaks. In my opinion, politically, he's disagreeable. But I cannot ignore him because he makes a claim as someone genuinely speaking, right? As opposed to blah, blah, blah, blah, blah.

And that's Auden: when we genuinely speak, the words aren't ready so it's a process of self-interruption which constantly is struggling against itself and therefore it needs some help. And where does this help come from? That's the muse, whatever the muse is; your muse.

KEVIN: So where does your help come from?

JUSTIN: To come back to you, at the final part of your question, is the problem of form. Sometimes forms are there, and whether ready-made in the form of couplets, or forms in the form of artificial algorithmic exercises, that's where help comes from, the rigours of form.

Pluraformity is the possibility of a muse which you reshape with your own content, or that you re-struggle with the form, or recreate the form from within it. That's a real muse. I'm perfectly happy with poets who say to me, *I have visitations from another world*. I don't fucking care where it comes from but there must be a muse or an absolutely Other that helps you to find those words or inspires those words, because if it's just you then it's not anybody.

KEVIN: How do you react when people say *what does that poem mean?*

JUSTIN: It's not really a meaningful question. Obviously it's a pragmatic and material question but poetry's bigger than those concerns. *Poetry* is both smaller and bigger a word than *creativity* to be honest. Creativity tries to bring poetry into a broad field of creativity, as just one of its aspects. Hence you can say, *what does this mean?*

Poetry tells you what creativity is; creativity isn't bigger than poetry. Poetry opens up the possibility. Poetry is a name for the origins of creativity. In which case, all questions you can ask about it are subordinates of poetry.

KEVIN: Sometimes when I'm preparing the undergraduate subject in poetry, all I really want to do is show them lots and lots of poems and hope that they get it without me having to do the lectures.

JUSTIN: That's really traditional. That traditional education is all over the world, as far as I can see, until very recently when it became the province of opportunistic technical goons, whether in ancient China or in Africa or in Europe, everyone's agreed.

Yeats says, *Nor is there singing school but studying. Monuments of its own magnificence.*[8] That's what the canon is. People who hate the canon don't know what they're talking about, right? There are many, many canons. The canon's always been plural and open. In fact, people who attack the canon are reactionary imbeciles. Why? Because they want to say, *that's just your feeling* or *that's just white middle class.*

No, the canon's been about going to look at the magnificence of this. What do you think? You don't have to like it, you just have to go, *wow; someone did something.* Or something did something there which made a claim on us and we don't know very much about it. I've spent my life reading this, here's a whole load of plural things, they're all different. Poetry is that difference, right?

I think that's the best mode. You show and you can say something about your apprehension of it. That's just one thing. The point is to get some way to transmit that thing.

KEVIN: Continuing then with the question of where material comes from, do you use conversations, anecdotes, things people do and say, do you take them over into your poetry? And how do you feel about it, if you do do that?

JUSTIN: I find a lot of prose fiction and creative nonfiction a very low genre. I find it cheap and opportunistic and narcissistic a lot of the time. And with its stupid claims to realism, I actually have a deep visceral reaction. Whereas, poets *can* do that but they don't. That's only one tiny aspect of what they do.

When I was writing *Bumf* I took an entire governmental report, a document spruiking the G20 and then improved it in every way. That can come from anywhere, but it's not the *place* that it comes from. The place that it comes from is crucial to the form that you make of it. You can't do that in poetry if you just take up bits . . . prose writers take it up and put it into whatever prose is, which is into a non-form. Sorry, I'm sounding very formalist. In prose it's just ah, ah, ah, ah, ah whereas poetry has to make the origin, or the place where those things came from, and the form that it gives *then*, it has to make those part of its form and also make its form part of its content. That's part of the poetic, the poetry. If it doesn't do that then it's just prose, one step above journalism, which doesn't mean it can't be very good; it's very important to have; but still.

KEVIN: I often read Helen Garner for the occasional brilliant sentence. And lots of prose writers for that reason.

JUSTIN: Yes, exactly

KEVIN: Does music play a role?

JUSTIN: I told you my feeling about wherever anything comes from, poetry transfigures it, right? And poetry is the transfiguration of the commonplace, can I say that? I'm sure someone said that, *transfiguration of the commonplace*.[9] It doesn't mean that I listen to music and think can I do that in verse or can I steal that? I think of the musicality of speech or writing rhythms. They should be part of the verse even if you break them with an ugliness or whatever. The musicality becomes one of the things you work with.

KEVIN: So continuing to pursue this question of the elements that go into production of poems, what role does mood play for you? For example, whether you sit down and write or not?

JUSTIN: If I had more time then mood would be more important, but now mood has to be subject to my stealing of time. Whatever my mood is, sometimes I obviously can't write. There's a mood thing and then there's a muse thing, if I can put it like that. Sometimes they come together, sometimes they don't.

KEVIN: Maybe there's something to be said for not having the time to wait for the mood.

JUSTIN: Yeah, exactly. Writer's block is a different thing when there's no time, you know? I think of all those early twentieth-century Russian poets like Mandelstam or Akhmatova. They're under fucking extreme social and political pressures and so they compose 'Stalin's fingers like ten fat worms'.[10] And they'd do it in their head and they'd relay them to other people who'd keep them in their head and memorise the poems of others in order to be written down or transmitted later.

KEVIN: I read a wonderful memoir of the Stalinist period where the author had memorised whole books of poetry, and she was standing in a queue and the local people knew that she had these books in her head. They said, *read us blah blah book* and she would start to read the book and then the guards would be looking for her book. They'd search and search for her book.

JUSTIN: Wow, that's awesome. In the ancient Greek mythology Mnemosyne—memory—is the mother of the muses. Without memory there's nothing. The memory has to be of the other, not just of the reader not just of the writer.

* * *

KEVIN: How quickly do you write?

JUSTIN: It depends, sometimes fast, sometimes slow. Some things deliberately can be written fast but take a decade and a half to construct, so *The Mundiad*. I write the couplets fast, as I said before, or sometimes or they come in little bursts because they have to, but then they're just like scritch, scritch, scritch and you assemble them later.

There's a lot of re-writing. There should have been more re-writing but one of the things about the project of *The Mundiad,* specifically, is it's now been published twice; it was first published in 2004 which was the first three books, then it was re-published as *The Mundiad* by John Hunter last year—with three extra books, but with no indication it had three extra books; like, it just gets bigger. The idea is that it just gets bigger and bigger and I re-write with every new iteration, as well. There's a lot of re-writing before it ever gets out, but now there's going to be lots of retrospective re-writing too. The whole thing should change and mutate even though it's exactly the same thing. There should be more re-writings, as I said before; some of it just doesn't work and I find that humiliating.

KEVIN: And you are in the process of doing that?

JUSTIN: Yes, I'm always in the process. When will it ever be done? That's in principle, the process of doing that. Whereas other things like palindromes, the intensity of how a palindrome is constructed personally, where you have to do it simultaneously from both ends, then make decisions about do you use words like *radar* or do you actually construct little semantic or syntactical bunches and add them in, or do you just do it as a big thing? The intensity of that, of having to do that process, is a different kind of re-writing or re-drafting because the rigours of the palindrome are a different kind of re-writing. Modalities of producing, in myself, the necessity, the unfortunate necessity, of different kinds of re-writing rather than just re-writing; there's many different kinds and some are retroactive and just evaluative, and others are prospective and just algorithmic.

KEVIN: And with *The Mundiad* is there a syllabic or metrical constriction to the lines?

JUSTIN: Yes, for the most part, they're heroic couplets, so iambic pentameter, first line and then the couplet with the rhyme at the end.

KEVIN: Your answers are so comprehensive that you've covered a number of these questions, and particularly, the question about *why* you stop writing and *when* you stop writing. Clearly you don't stop writing . . .

JUSTIN: No, even when I'm not writing.

KEVIN: . . . and the process is the process.

JUSTIN: Even when you're not writing, you're writing; or when you're writing, you're not writing. It's such a complex thing.

KEVIN: Let's go on to the last question which is maybe the strangest question of the interview, is there anything your readers owe you?

JUSTIN: This is a strange question. I'd just like a few readers at all. Jacques Derrida says, about James Joyce, noone's ever really read *Ulysses* and *Finnegans Wake* properly. Unreadable, in principle. But at the beginning no one fucking knew who Joyce was; he probably had about six or seven readers, but they were very good readers. It's not that my readers owe me. Are there readers, really? Part of being a poet today is having to generate your own readers under extreme conditions.

KEVIN: Your own half a dozen readers?

JUSTIN: Your own half a dozen reasons. Maybe they're there, maybe they're not. Sometimes your friends read it, sometimes other poets read it. This is where the reading writing thing is so weird. Do they actually read it? Or, *yeah, I liked your book* or, *Yeah, I'll pay some lip service*. There's all sorts of reasons why people read, but do people read? Read in the sense of, something here I haven't seen before? You have to provide that to your readers and that's not up to you to say. Only your readers can say that.

But no one owes me anything. If I'm going to be a poet in that honorific, we have to give people the possibility to find something that they wouldn't otherwise find. It's not up to you to dictate that.

KEVIN: I think that's a great answer for an almost unanswerable question.

JUSTIN: All a bit paradoxical. It is interesting to think about these things and I'm trying to answer these questions in a form of genuine speaking, if that makes sense?

KEVIN: I'm sure you had a think about these things but when we come to the live event it's not quite the same as it is on the page.

JUSTIN: No, it's not quite that. I had a look at them and I thought about them, but I didn't want to de-genuine-ify them.

NOTES

1   Tony Birch is a Melbourne-based writer, author of a number of books including the prose collections *Shadowboxing* (2006), *Father's Day* (2009), and *The Promise* (2014). His poetry collection, *Broken Teeth*, was published by Cordite Books in 2016

2   Clemens, Justin 2004 *The Mundiad*, Melbourne: Black Inc

3   Carroll, Lewis 1983 [1871] 'Jabberwocky', in *The Random House Book of Poetry for Children*, selected by Jack Prelutsky, New York: Random House

4   Clemens, Justin 2014 'Odeur Gee Twin Tee Breeze Bane Twin Tee For', in *Bumf*, edited by Jeremy Poxon, Sally Olds, Stuart Glover and Cosima McGrath. http://bumf.com.au/index.php

5   George Steiner, speaking with journalist Wim Kayzer in 2007 about what he learned from his father's foresight in escaping the Nazis: 'Wherever I go, my homeland is a typewriter or a pen. If I'm allowed that, I have my passport'. (See https://www.youtube.com/watch?v=iA5gTD69imI, 16 July 2007)

6   John Forbes 2001 'Death, an Ode', in *Collected Poems, 1970–1998*, Blackheath: Brandl and Schlesinger

7   In his introduction to the 1935 anthology, *The Poet's Tongue*, edited by WH Auden and John Garrett, London: George Bell and Sons

8   Yeats, WB 1933 'Sailing to Byzantium', in *The Poems of WB Yeats: A New Edition*, edited by Richard J Finneran, London: Macmillan Publishing

9   *Transfiguration of the Commonplace* is the title of a book by art critic and philosopher Arthur C Danto. Subtitled *A philosophy of art*, it is published by Harvard University Press, 1983

10 Osip Mandelstam (1891–1938) wrote a satirical poem called 'The
   Stalin epigram' (1933), which he read to a few friends, including Anna
   Akhmatova; his arrest and exile is attributed to that poem, which includes
   the lines: 'Kremlin mountaineer, / the ten thick worms his fingers / his
   words like measures of weight, / the huge laughing cockroaches on his top
   lip . . .' See Carolyn Forché (ed), *Against Forgetting: Twentieth-Century Poetry
   of Witness* (trans WS Merwin and Clarence Brown), New York: WW Norton
   & Co, 1989

"Watching how thoughts move"
Ken Bolton

Australian Experimental Arts Foundation, Adelaide, South Australia

JEN: I wondered about your connections to the everyday world. What is it that keeps you out of the world of words and connected back to the world in which we live?

KEN: Well, words are my handle on things, the way I can explain things to myself. Formulations about the world—that you test in your brain and then on the page: they are my way of understanding the world and demonstrating to myself that I've got a handle on some aspect of it. It's really just a matter of seeing and thinking.

JEN: George Steiner talks with the heartbreak of a failed Christian, or a Christian who sees the world failing, about the gap that has appeared between word and world.[1] It sounds as though you actually bridge that gap yourself.

KEN: Words are a code. It's probably fashionable to say that, or something like it. We don't know how much more connected to things words were for people in previous ages. As soon as someone (as Eliot did[2]) nominates the seventeenth century or the fifteenth century as an ideal time of less alienation, somebody else is usually able to indicate that word and world weren't so closely knitted together at that time either.

JEN: Or that those people were not naïve, perhaps.

KEN: Or not as naïve or unexamined as Steiner (whom I haven't read) thinks. It's a golden age he's creating. It doesn't matter to me that word and world are not the same thing. This is not stuff I think much about.

JEN: In your writing life—which has spanned several decades now—what sustains you?

KEN: Bananas? Well, I enjoy writing. I would probably not feel as though I was paying attention to my life if I weren't doing it. It is the way that I pay attention.

JEN: So the examined life for you is that of poetry, or in poetry?

KEN: Yes, although on the other hand, at the same time I do sometimes think that my examinations aren't all that deep. It might as easily be said that the lies I tell to myself about my life are necessary to me.

I enjoy thinking, sometimes, and if you're a verbal person thinking is your only recourse. I don't have any political power, I can't make anything else happen in my life. In a way, of course, it's just talking behind the world's back.

JEN: Talking behind the world's back? That's a mildly subversive approach to the world. And of course you're organising things like the Lee Marvin readings,[3] and that has to be a valuable thing for other poets?

KEN: Sure, well I hope so.

JEN: Several people have mentioned it, and mentioned it with real warmth.

KEN: Good. I put a lot into making the readings work—but it's also done vaguely for commercial purposes. I need the shop to survive. That's a reason too.

I also wanted a reading that I would feel comfortable reading at myself. If you create an audience of people who are interested in each other's work and paying attention to it, then you can benefit from it yourself as a reader.

JEN: Do you remember where and when it was that you first encountered poetry?

KEN: Probably in primary school, but I don't think I paid attention to it then.

JEN: There's not that moment where you thought *oh, my God, that's a poem.*

KEN: No. I remember liking it at high school, largely because I was good at talking about it. It was the standard stuff, John Donne and TS Eliot, Hopkins.

JEN: Everyone that they teach us about when we're 12, 13, 14.

KEN: It was more like 15, 16. I began to think, *this is interesting.* I thought I might be a novelist and I wrote bad, short novels featuring the kids in the class as anti-heroes; they were comic things. Then I went to university. And although I thought about novels, I never came up with any plot, really, that I could take off with. I didn't start writing poetry until I was 21, 22.

JEN: So the short image of the poem, that intensity of a poem, works for you but not that long marathon of a novel. I'd like to be able to look inside brains and see why is it that some people must write novels and other people must write poems.

KEN: I've been able to write them with a friend, John Jenkins, whom I collaborated with on a couple of verse novels and one prose novel, so it's not that I *can't* do it, it's just there's not as much interest in it for me.[4]

JEN: So you started reading poetry at high school; are you still a regular reader? And mostly poetry?

KEN: No, I read poetry a bit. Mostly the same people over and over again. I read some continental philosophy, not always liking it or appreciating it properly, but I do. Barthes, Foucault, Adorno, Benjamin, and Sloterdijk. I read art criticism a bit and a lot of cultural commentary.

JEN: Do you describe yourself as a poet—would that be the way you'd identify yourself to a stranger?

KEN: If you're going to say *poet* someone's going to raise their eyebrow. You're almost certainly going to have to answer further questions like *what do you write?* Most people don't particularly want to meet a poet. Generally I say I run a bookshop, if asked.

JEN: As a poet, is there a descriptor that you'd add to that, a *something* poet?

KEN: No. I'm aware that I'm an Australian poet because I'm thinking a lot of the time about Western European culture—its concepts and terminology, its history, its art. I know the degree to which I do and don't fit in there. And the degree to which 'we' don't fit in, Australians.

JEN: Australian—not lyric or wry or anything else?

KEN: I hate the word wry and . . . no, I'm not a lyrical poet. I happen to be an Australian poet.

JEN: Some of your poetry strikes me as socially critical or politically critical. Do you consciously see poetry as a way of exploring social/political issues?

KEN: Well it comes up because it is what I'm thinking about. Why would you write about things you weren't thinking about—but also, if pressed, I'd say it seems to me terrible that a lot of contemporary poetry is not especially relevant to anybody . . . or it's nature poetry of a sort that's hardly needs eco-consciousness, or it's poetry that feels that its topicality is a stamp of approval—that it wears and doesn't have to earn.

JEN: Do you mean that it's not actually thinking, or even manoeuvring? It's just saying, *there's a tree and we don't look after trees well.*

KEN: You can stand, pretty uselessly—and many do—beside any current agenda, yes. And a lot of other people write poetry that consists of shrugging *'Poetry, it's irrelevant—and yet we're doing it! Ha ha'.* I couldn't demonstrate that poetry is relevant but I do like the eighteenth-century thinking that you could write science or philosophy as poetry. I mean, while I don't like very much Augustan poetry really, I like the ambitions that it had and the fact that it hadn't agreed to go quietly to the small room, as an adjunct to literature, real literature.

* * *

JEN: Going back to you; you grew up in Sydney; did you go to university in Sydney?

KEN: I did; I grew up in Sydney and went to university there.

JEN: And of course you've been living in Adelaide for quite a long time.

KEN: Since 1982.

JEN: Do you find that the place informs your writing, or that your writing is inflected by being at home, being at work, travelling, living in different places?

KEN: Well, I pay attention to light and textures. I pay attention to family and the life I lead here, centred mostly in the visual arts—the ambitions of particular people, careers beginning and kicking on for a while and changing; I pay attention to that. But a lot of the time, really, I'm just reading books—that are published elsewhere. I happen to be reading them in Adelaide, that's all.

JEN: In your own poetic practice what part is played by your relationships with other poets? Are you a solitary poet, or do you feel that you need the company of others?

KEN: When I began as a young poet in Sydney there was the excitement of scenes and factions, and of groups that were related but not entirely accepting of each other. I thought that was terribly interesting and exciting and I was all for it.

When I came to Adelaide, though, I was happy to be subsumed into the visual arts. I don't (or did not till very recently) connect with writers much. I'm mostly connected to old friends from the past, people like Pam Brown and Laurie Duggan.[5] We email regularly. Their epistolary friendship is important to me—perhaps more important to me than it is for them. They play a large part in my life.

JEN: The writing sector, whether that's bookstores, publishers, writers groups and so on: how significant is that in the development of your poetic practice and its ongoing character?

KEN: I always wanted the poems published. In the 1980s it looked like I wasn't going to be published much at all, and that was definitely depressing. I thought what I was writing was okay so I decided to keep going.

A lack of support can have an effect on you. I've been lucky in being published though not usually published to a great acclaim or critical reception. Some people might like the work. I haven't sold large numbers of books.

JEN: Very few poets do of course.

KEN: No, not usually unless you're on a syllabus or something.

JEN: Do you send early drafts of your work to your friends to comment on?

KEN: Yes; mostly by email now.

JEN: So you're workshopping your poems with others?

KEN: Not workshopping. You don't want to make more work for your friends than they're prepared to do. Usually you expect people to say *yes* or *no* or *I prefer these ones rather than these others*—of the four or five poems you might send. That's all I'm asking for. Specific things will get mentioned, approved or worried over, and some proofreading occurs.

I'm happy to do the same for them as long as they'll promise me that they won't take my advice without thinking about it pretty hard:

usually I can see, as soon as I've made a change, that you could make other changes, or that the original is just as good. Sometimes I will write alternative phrasings for certain parts of something Laurie or Pam has written and they'll often take a quarter or a third of that on board—which is more than I expect.

JEN: How do you feel if they seem to be disappointed, or not interested, in what you've written?

KEN: I don't mind really because lately I'm writing so much. I'm not heartbroken.

JEN: If they think it's adequate or not really that good, are they usually right?

KEN: Usually, between them, they are. Sometimes they have quite different views.

* * *

JEN: I have a quote from Auden, from his TS Eliot Memorial Lectures. He said, *when we genuinely speak we do not have the words ready to do our bidding, we have to find them, we do not know exactly what we are going to say until we've said it and we say and hear something new that's never been said or heard before.* It's an idea of genuinely speaking and trying to find words to do our bidding. Does that resonate with you?

KEN: Sure. I imagine both Auden and Eliot would find my usage very slack from their points of view. I wouldn't suggest that I struggle hard to find the perfect word. My phrasing is much more colloquial, looser. But you do find that you've said something you hadn't thought of before, though not often that *nobody's* thought before.

JEN: But fresh for you.

KEN: Fresh enough.

JEN: What are the processes you use to 'find words to do your bidding'?

KEN: My bidding? I almost don't know how to answer that. I start writing. The words are like an extendable prop . . . that I'm construct-ing and using as a stick. I'm poking a stick at concepts. Is 'proleptic' the word?

I often start with a list of things I'm thinking about. *I've ordered a cup of coffee* or *I've stubbed my toe* sort of thing, or *someone unusual has come into the coffee shop*. If I've got those three things on the page I add a fourth and it sometimes turns into a sentence and then the sentence will begin, begin to 'negotiate' with these things.

Usually I'll begin almost without thinking about it. It certainly isn't Auden's scrutinising of particular words and rejecting them. I'm more interested in finding a break that gives suddenly, and I'm through and in and I've started without thinking about it almost.

JEN: This image, this event: it gives you a starting point and then the ideas that emerge out of that?

KEN: A lot of them will be ideas you've had in your head for a couple of weeks, or just half an hour before, that are allowed onto the page now, by the occasion. And then you might think of something 'orig-inal' as well.

I'm interested in watching how thoughts move and what kind of pat-terns and shapes they take, what associations they allow or disallow. Or allow in a friendly way, or which they fight with; because you can have a number of registers going in a poem and there might be a main register, which will acknowledge the other register as different but will somehow accommodate it. All of that is what I'm interested in.

JEN: Are there critical voices that you rely on? These might be people in your own network or long dead poets: I see you cite Frank O'Hara from time to time in your work for instance. Are they in your head sometimes as critical voices looking at what you've written?

KEN: In terms of O'Hara, he extends real attitudes about writing that I am sympathetic to, and occasionally I allow him to be over my shoulder looking at what I'm writing.

Often you've got to defend your work from influence. O'Hara's pretty sharp, and if I can't be as sharp as that am I meant to pack up shop, you know? Other writers will stand—for me—for their particular kind of attitude. And I've probably internalised, or feel I have, Laurie and Pam, so I might have an idea of them—as reading my stuff over my shoulder—and disapproving or saying *There's a fair bit of fat in that sentence, Ken, to be cut.* But apart from them, no—just the art criticism that formed my thinking at some stage and stayed there: things that the 1960s and the early 1970s produced around the various arguments happening then—mostly to do with expressionism versus minimalism and literalism. The minimalists and their attitude to the painters of the previous generation—and the artists themselves, Robert Morris and others. I like reading them. And I think about visual arts all the time, because I write a lot of art criticism. It's my writing as an art critic that keeps those people's ideas and attitudes alive for me.

JEN: You were talking about your poetic practice as a combination of ideas and momentary observations or thoughts, but I wondered about mood: do you have to be in the right mood to compose? Is there an emotional element?

KEN: No, I don't have to be, which I know because occasionally I force myself to write a poem—because it's just been a while—and those poems often turn out to be okay.

JEN: So there's no muse touching you on the shoulder and saying, *now, now.*

KEN: No, no. Sometimes you feel like writing because you're in a good mood or mentally limber—that's the only way I could describe it. It doesn't always produce stuff—or often the first poem it produces is no good anyway. It's the second one or the third one. It might begin with your being quite bored. I don't require a particular mood. I can write at any time.

JEN: In so far as there is an element of emotion in poetry, in your poetry, would that be you, Ken, or the voice of the poem itself, or is it a sort of emotion that might be generated in your readers, if we could break it up in those three ways?

KEN: I don't know. I don't need to know, and perhaps I need not to know in fact.

I like to be funny and to use logic. I think the best thinkers are funny. There's nobody I'd take seriously as a thinker who doesn't make good jokes, including Adorno. If you're thinking about categories, and you're thinking about culture, and about other people's propositions, obviously you're going to make witticisms and jokes as the fastest and shortest cut.

JEN: How about the speed of your composition: are you a fast writer?

KEN: I think so, probably. I stop quite often, but not to do Auden's job of searching hard for the right word; it would be to let more ideas come, or because a line of thought had stopped.

JEN: And so you leave it until it emerges or something else happens.

KEN: It's a matter of changing the record that's playing, or looking around the room. You'll get a second thought.

JEN: Do you write to music?

KEN: I often have it on but I'm not rigorous about it. It helps the time move and I like music.

JEN: So you don't think *I must have Faure playing if I'm going to write like this?*

KEN: No, no. It's probably The Velvet Underground or John Coltrane. And often the same record over and over and over again—because you don't want to pay attention to it, and you don't want a *change* of mood.

New music is never any good for my writing. You inevitably pay attention to it. I write to music that I've got used to.

JEN: So putting on some John Coltrane, that familiarity, gives you . . . is that a cocoon? Is that what forms the cocoon?

KEN: Yeah, or The Velvet Underground. For about a decade it was James Brown.

JEN: That's pretty energetic music. Carrying on with the ideas of composing poets: do you see composing and editing as the same process, or do you feel differently about the two, do you think differently when you're in those two stages?

KEN: You edit as you compose. They're mixed up. Once you feel that most of it is written you'll go back and do more editing. You hope to edit as though you're a stranger to the poem, so you need to have left the poem for a while.

JEN: So you will cellar your draft, your almost-finished draft.

KEN: I do. It's very hard to walk away from stuff that's still interesting to you. I sometimes work on a poem too much and too long, too soon after it's written. So walking away is a good idea. Ideally, leave it for a while if you can, and edit it more coldly. Though sometimes that cold edit is not sympathetic enough to the poem: you can do damage to the poem. Or, there might not be much you *can* do, except obvious things. Still, some of those things are worth doing, and sometimes the obvious things you're doing don't become obvious very quickly. For instance, a useful inversion of a word order might not strike me for six months or a year. Even though I've come back to the poem, supposedly cold, four or five times in that year, I will still not have seen the obvious thing to do. So I'm not actually good at it. But you've got to at least remove the spelling mistakes.

Basically it is written fairly quickly, in a couple of long bursts—with a bit of fitful kicking on. And then the rest of the editing is small scale. I'm not very good at making major cuts. I've seen other people do it very well and I wish that I could. Sometimes I change poems quite a lot in terms how they look on the page. I might decide to make it in two line stanzas rather than just a block or in threes or fours, and see how it goes. Usually it changes the pace of the poem, and that can suit some parts well and others less so. All this is usually well after the poem is there on the page.

JEN: When a poem is ready to go to a publisher, what is it about that process that makes you say *yeah, I'm done with this now?* Do you have a sense of being conscious that that poem is ready to see the world?

KEN: Not in any mystical or aesthetic way. Sometimes the poem is ready quickly; some poems, if they're longer, will have more areas that are slightly problematic. I might figure I'm never going to get all of them exactly perfect so it's a matter of trade-offs.

It involves reading the poem often enough for you to be in it and feel that you know how the whole poem works, not just the problem stanza. There's nothing very magical about it really; it's just editing.

But choosing to publish? If you want to send a poem off you'll find one to send off. You might be sending it too early or not; it's a different discipline.

JEN: Do you think in sentences, or do you think in lines; or do you start a sentence and then think about the line after you've got your sentence right?

KEN: You launch sentences or propositions often before you know what the whole of the proposition is or where it's going. You have the animus that has begun the proposition; it is tending towards one direction or hoping that it's going one way. I start prospective sentences, but the writing progresses by phrase or by line. They have a weight to them, they lean in a direction, they seek to go in a particular direction. Then the poem is the interesting enterprise, or the adventure: of seeing what you're going to say.

Often a poem that finally gets published, and that has a lot of narrow lines, say, will have begun as long lines on the handwritten page. This *should* cast doubt on a very confident answer to your question about *do you begin with phrases or lines or sentences*. I just begin. I want them to be sentences and I expect they will be, but often my sentences, if they're long, don't have a terribly strong or coherent grammatical centre to them or muscle to them. I'd rather they did have but they don't always. So sometimes the sentences peter out, interestingly I hope; they peter out, gesturing at a couple of directions they may have gone but didn't get to.

A poem for me is an initial impulse, followed up by a lot of correction and kicking-on, or of choice between possible directions. I'm writing for myself in the initial sense. (So I'm not talking down to a reader.) Ideally I've done my best by the original impulse and idea.

NOTES

1   Steiner, George 1989 *Real Presences: Is There Anything in What We Say?*, London: Faber & Faber

2   Eliot, TS, 'The Metaphysical Poets', first published in *Times Literary Supplement*, 20 October 1921; republished in *Selected Essays 1917–1932*, New York: Harcourt, Brace and Co, 1932 (241–50)

3   The Lee Marvin Readings series, a venue for readings in Adelaide, operating since the 1990s

4   Bolton, Ken and John Jenkins 1988 *Airborne Dogs and Other Collaborations* Melbourne: Brunswick Hills Press; 1989 *The Ferrara Poems: A Novel*, Adelaide: Experimental Art Foundation; 1993 *The Gutman Variations*, North Adelaide: South Australian Publications Ventures and Futures; 2001 *The Wallah Group*, Adelaide: Little Esther Books; 2002 *Nutters Without Fetters*, Berry: Press Press; 1994 'Gwendolyn Windswept', in *Otis Rush 9*: 177-99; 2005 *Poems of Relative Unlikelihood*, Adelaide: Little Esther Books

5   Pam Brown, an Australian poet who was for many years poetry editor at *Overland* journal; Laurie Duggan, Australian poet, translator and editor

"Let the poem call the shots"
Michael Sharkey

Castlemaine, Victoria

KEVIN: Michael, let's start from the assumption that any poet is connected to the world. What are your points of connection to the world?

MICHAEL: Just about everything you can think of.

KEVIN: And which ones matter to you?

MICHAEL: I suppose people, in the sense of what's going on around me at the moment, in the neighbourhood, the natural and built environment. The way people live, the way society's structured; that involves connection with news, current affairs, history.

KEVIN: Those connections provide you with subject matter, content, themes?

MICHAEL: Well, subject matter. I don't know about themes; themes seem to run a little deeper. Consciousness, the usual existential things: *what are we doing here?* We're alive; it won't be much fun being dead. But we won't know anything about that, so the phenomenon of people's worry about death is curious to me.

KEVIN: What has sustained you in your writing life?

MICHAEL: That was probably the hardest one of the lot. Well, it's the fact that you just keep going. It's like something I can't help, like hearing music or listening to things or having sight. What sustains it?

Curiosity might be one way of putting it, a sense of wonder that we behave as we do, that we continue to do that, the things that have been written and done so many times, but you can't help doing it—so, the curiosity about repetition and pattern.

KEVIN: Could you have chosen not to continue to write?

MICHAEL: I could have. At times I have, but it's frustrating, because it's as natural as formulating a thought or an idea. It's as natural as speech or as breathing. Try holding your breath for twenty minutes and it's the same effect as trying to say, *I won't write.* There are lull periods of course, ebbs and flows and getting preoccupied with other things.

KEVIN: Would you say that a habit of writing has sustained you?

MICHAEL: It could be a habit, but it's not as mechanical as, *Every day I must write a poem*—like Kit Kelen or certain other people who insist on knocking out 365 things a year.[1] I can't do that, but I can scribble things every day and pile them all up and then edit them and see if there's a poem there from time to time. I wouldn't say that I frequently sit down and consciously dash off a poem.

*   *   *

KEVIN: Can you remember where you first encountered poetry?

MICHAEL: Probably when I heard it from older people: my mother, schoolteachers in primary school, my father. When did I first read it? Probably in old-fashioned primary or kids' books, things that were virtually nursery rhymes and songs and folkish things.

KEVIN: Did your mother and father have poems off by heart?

MICHAEL: My mother and father were both good at that, and as time went on they kept on knowing more. My father especially, because he changed career from being a farmer to a science teacher to a teacher of history and English and classics. He taught Greek and Roman history, and Japanese and Chinese history, and he was interested in the literatures of those places. He had a good ear for languages. He could tell the story of the Three Bears in Burmese, things like that. And he warmed to Blake and Coleridge and Donne; he could recite reams of stuff. That was when I was moving into my teens. By then I'd read a lot of stuff in local libraries and what was on the shelf. My mother had an aunt who was a teacher, and she had lots of old editions of Burns and Longfellow and Browning. So you just read them, because they were there, like you read everything as a kid.

KEVIN: When did you start writing poetry?

MICHAEL: I started to write things when I was 13, 14, 15. I wrote a play, thinking that would go on. It was set somewhere in medieval times about a writer—a student and student behaviour. I was reading lots of fabliaux and medieval things. We had Chaucer on the shelf, so I read Chaucer long before I left school. That was good fun. I was taken up by that whole English medieval lyric and narrative tradition. And my mother probably had read lots of stories to me.

I remember when I was very young I had book after book on the shelf. Almost every Christmas or birthday, I'd get a book of stories and poems and fables about Greece or Turkey or Russia or other places. It was great fun, that; and reading the *Tanglewood Tales*.[2] So I grew up in this mythic double world of my parents' knowledge and of what was happening out there. Just about everyone in the family could recite stuff. My grandmother was a musician and other people in the family were musicians so they always had songs going on.

KEVIN: If you were to describe yourself to a stranger, would you be likely to identify yourself as a poet?

MICHAEL: Yeah. Now I would.

KEVIN: When you were working as an academic, would you have?

MICHAEL: No. It seemed no one was interested. There were no such things as creative writing schools when I went to university. It was all hard stuff, literature, languages. I never went near workshops. People didn't walk around saying *I am a poet*. Certain people I was introduced to earlier were poets, even before I went to university. I was conscious of Roland Robinson as someone who'd married one of my father's cousins, and I'd read his poems.[3] That relationship was looked at a bit askance in the family because of his reputation as a womaniser. I ran into Robert Graves when I worked for a publisher in Sydney in 1967. I was very conscious of him as a poet, the first I'd ever met live, in fact. Some years later, Leonie Kramer introduced Alec Hope and others to a class I was in at Sydney, and I thought, *Well, he's a poet*. I mean, it was incidental that he was a professor, or whatever he was, he just struck us as a poet, his reputation was huge. I never called myself a poet in that sort of company.

KEVIN: But now you feel more comfortable?

MICHAEL: Well, now it's more or less my occupation, it's all I do. I edit poems, I read poems, I write poems. I think you have to face it at some stage, so that's what I do.

KEVIN: And when people say to you, *what kind of poet are you*, do you add descriptors?

MICHAEL: No. The only time I add a descriptor is if I'm introducing myself to someone overseas. Generally I've been invited there, so they already know—I don't have to say what sort of poet I am because some people have read the stuff, or they'll find out.

KEVIN: I feel as if it's more fraught to try to describe what kind of poet you are than to describe what kind of fiction writer you might be, because it's not so much fitting into a set of conventions as moving into competing schools of thought in poetry.

MICHAEL: People have called me a satiric poet and at times comic, but I don't think that works for me. I think I just work as an observer, and elegy is something that I'm more at home with. Lyric, elegy, balladic stuff; I like narrative in a poem. I think, if I write satiric stuff, it doesn't qualify me to call myself a satirist; that's a misreading or a shortcut.

KEVIN: I feel that too about your poetry. So, does poetry provide you with ways to engage with social and political issues?

MICHAEL: Yes, certainly does. It can't help but do that.

KEVIN: I guess it engages with those issues differently to the way prose would or letters or articles.

MICHAEL: It does. It aims to compress and to compare things. If I read a lot of history, which I do, and a lot of classics, which I do, I can't help thinking it's all beyond a twice told tale. Certain things are clichés. Like, we're at war again, aren't we, this week, and what can you say about it that hasn't been said? And even to say that we're at war in the same place with the same people is clichéd. You've got to be good at coming up with something new. That old question of *make it new* always depended, to me, on what *it* was that you were making new, as much as a way of *saying* it again.[4] So to *make it new*, I thought the *it* had better be important, had better be something that's life and death. The fact that everyone appears to fall in love with someone and then sometimes fall out of love—so what? The stories exist, they're in the world around you, but how do you connect them in some way that doesn't bore you witless? I get really annoyed with myself if I write a cliché. I think everything connects with the world, but I think poetry should somehow say it in less space than prose or more excitingly.

KEVIN: Do you set out to write political poems?

MICHAEL: I have done at times, to see that it can be done. It's like Shelley's *Masque of Anarchy*;[5] it's a squib you toss off, but you don't take it too seriously. If you write something and you're really angry, you'd better not let the anger take over from the craft.

I was at one time writing ballads about the Falklands War; it can be done, but I don't think much of it as poetry. I don't think many people write good political poetry.

KEVIN: So there's a difference between the political poem and poems that tackle political issues?

MICHAEL: I think there is. Any poem can tackle politics at some level. A lot of people tend to think of the profoundest love poetry as tackling politics of personal affairs and intimate relations. You've got to be as good as Horace or Catullus or Tibullus, people who could run through a gamut of emotions from initial allure through to obsession and to all the frustrations and anger and contempt. That comes into writing about politics too. I mean, I feel contempt for my cowardice; I should be doing more things out there, but I lack the courage. You tell yourself you lack the occasion, but you don't.

Poetry that engages with things: I like the longer poems that have been written because they do tackle issues like rule and subjection, and leadership and loyalty, and courage.

*   *   *

KEVIN: You've moved home recently. Does that affect your writing—the location that you're in, and moving locations?

MICHAEL: It has to, always.

KEVIN: And do you know how it affects your writing?

MICHAEL: I want to know more about the area, the district, what goes on here, what's happened here, and get to know the ropes. That happens whether you travel somewhere for a month or two or three. You've had the experience as well, of travelling to places where you've propped for months or several months, and so have I, and I'm fascinated: that's my initial reaction, just, *Oh, this is wonderful, this is totally different*—and then a kind of twinge, that I've neglected to stay in touch with people left behind. But that happens anyway; it happens the minute you leave home as a kid, although not too many people seem to leave home nowadays. When I change address, I'm curious about everything, the weather, the climate, the soil, everything. Natural habitat, you know.

KEVIN: What does that do to your poetry?

MICHAEL: It weaves its way in as you start using a slightly different frame of reference, but it's almost unconscious.

KEVIN: Are you writing about different things since you've been here?

MICHAEL: It's changed in some directions. I was already thinking in a different way before I left. I was tired of everything associated with the older routine, anxious to get away from that university and the day-to-day routine of meetings, committees, and listening to people complaining about what life was like. I didn't want to know about it, I just wanted to get over the initial shock of having freedom, and then to rearrange things.

First was an immense purging of things I wanted to get rid of. I thought, *do I keep all of those lecture notes?* Probably not. *Do I keep some of them?* Yes, probably. *Do I keep all those notebooks?* Let's have a look and see if there is anything there; I'll tear out *that* page, keep *that*, keep *that*, throw *that*. There's an immense amount of ditching stuff, and then out of change I decided I'd got tired of my own habits and in every sense wanted to try something else.

KEVIN: I suppose it's not just a question of changing location, is it? It's a question of ending a career and entering into a new phase of life.

MICHAEL: Everything does change and it's not just a career change as such, because I have no career apart from writing and thinking about books and reading, and seeing how other people do it, and revising everything I ever thought about poetry.

I go back to looking at rhetoric in a way I wasn't able to before. I'm fascinated by the origins of things like metre in poetry, so I'm reading a lot more medieval poetry and theory than I ever used to and a lot more early poetry, and a lot more poetry in other languages.

KEVIN: Do you think you can hear metre in that early poetry?

MICHAEL: I think so. Especially from a background of listening to metrical things—Longfellow, Tennyson, and Browning and people who had a really good ear. And all the songs and church stuff too. I was brought up in a tradition where there were hymns and things, boring as bat shit the way they were sung quite often, but interesting words to read on a page and to see how they fell out. There was stress and metre and rhyme going on in Church Latin. That predisposes me now to want to go back and look at things like those medieval poems, and those before, and track it right down the line, back to where Latin becomes rhythmic and harmonious.

I could spend time reading a book or a stunningly good chapter all day and thinking about it—and not wanting to immediately put it into practice. Then thinking, *God I've got a lot of padding in my poem*, so I need to go through and strike out everything that looks like a superfluous adjective or adverb. I agonise still about how many question marks I can build into a poem.

KEVIN: Yes, I noticed there's a lot of questions in your poems. And wonderful questions.

MICHAEL: Yeah, I think they're all dialogic. Questions, like silence, are terrific things to have in a poem; gaps between the expressions.

KEVIN: When you do that kind of editing, I'm assuming from reading your poems that you have not a strict metrical pattern you're working to, but always a music to your lines. So when you go down to eliminating adjectives or adverbs, what happens to the rhythmic poem?

MICHAEL: A different rhythm comes in and it's more of a contrapuntal thing. One line says this, the next line appears to be saying something else, the third line will pick up something that was in one of the two up above. I'm using a lot more rhyme than I used to, but I'm using it in a different way.

107

KEVIN: Do you sometimes leave your adjectives and adverbs where they are for the sake of rhythm?

MICHAEL: I don't like to, but they insist sometimes and stay there, don't they? It's difficult to be hard and fast about that because you let the poem call the shots. If you try to force it, it'll sound forced. I'd much rather have the thing sound as if it's a human being speaking than something mechanical. I don't mind chopped, if the reader can follow the bouncing ball and jump from point to point. I think that's the way I like poetry, not to tell everything, but just to leave a lot of imaginative gaps.

KEVIN: So to continue the question of stylistics and rhetoric and rhythm, how relevant do you think a person's education is to the type of poetry they end up writing?

MICHAEL: One hundred per cent, in my case, but I don't know that this is the case with everyone.

KEVIN: I suppose the assumption that lies behind that question is that poetry is not a natural expression, it's an expression that arises out of a culture and its education system.

MICHAEL: It's probably true; we're acculturated according to a whole lot of things: early childhood influences and references. The language we're brought up in sets up a rhythm in us and we can't get over that. You can try to be bilingual, trilingual; some people can do this very well; they can switch.

I've just been reading the interview with Herta Müller, who got the Nobel Prize not so long back.[6] She can speak several languages: German, Yiddish, Romanian, et cetera. She talks about going back to pick up Romanian, and finding that when she's writing, sometimes she'll reach for a German word or some other word because it fits—I just love that facility. Plenty of other people can do that. I think it is a matter of acculturation, but most of us are monoglots, and we're brought up in families where the rhythms of speech reflect everything, class and education.

KEVIN: What about your relationships with other poets—what kind of influence has that had on you?

MICHAEL: Immense, because my relationships with other poets have been, by and large, with what they've written rather than what I've heard. I don't go to many poetry readings; I don't enjoy them, as a rule. I'm subjected to a lot of stuff that's just excruciatingly bad.

I go to things because I'm curious about a particular person, as a rule. Or I've heard something or read something of theirs and I wonder what they're doing now. Especially if it's a gap of years. I am influenced by other people. I read a lot and I subscribe to a lot of things. I look at the 'poem of the day' on the web when I remember.

Tomorrow a friend from New Zealand is going to drop in here for a day or two. That's going to be nice because he and his wife I've known for years, and he writes biographies, and I do too. We've stayed in touch by letter over the last thirty years. I can sound things out with him, or we talk about all sorts of rubbish in the world, not always poetry. I know the sort of poetry he writes, and if it doesn't really appeal to me we can workshop everyone else we know. 'What do you think about this?' we ask each other.

KEVIN: You don't workshop each other?

MICHAEL: No, not really, I don't really do that with many people at all.

KEVIN: Is there anyone who reads your drafts and comments on them?

MICHAEL: I will float them past two or three people whose ears I sort of trust.

KEVIN: Is Winifred one of those?

MICHAEL: On occasion; not often. I would sooner try other women friends, because they'll tell me if I've struck a bum-note as well as she can, yet I don't have that element of personality and intimacy in there, and I prefer that.

I remember the criticism that Bishop and Lowell traded backwards and forwards: I think that was sensible. They weren't lovers or anything like that, so she could be pretty brutal on his confessional streak and he could be pretty brutal on certain impulses in her work.

KEVIN: And she learned her editing skills from Marianne Moore.

MICHAEL: That's right, and I picked up some from other people. I used to float stuff up to Grace Perry, who was editing *Poetry Australia* years ago. She would always say, *This is rubbish, why don't you write in the twentieth century; where are you*, and *Get modern*, and things like that, which was awfully useful.

Les Murray was someone else. He was a writer in residence at the University of New England, about 1978, and I found him an affable sort of a bloke to talk to. On other things, his attitudes I find appalling, but he's terrifically knowledgeable about poetry and different languages. Very sociable, and can be quite abruptly dismissive of things. He'd say to me, *Have you got anything I can publish?* That was when he was co-editing *Poetry Australia*. I'd send him a couple of things, and he'd say, *I'll take that* straight off. I appreciate that ruthlessness.

I'll do the same thing with poets that I'm editing. I'll say, *I like that; I'll take it*, or *Drop the last line and you've got a good poem*. They'll come back and say, *I can't do that*, and I'll say, *Okay, I can't take it* or *Oh well, I'll bend the rules*.

KEVIN: Do they more often than not make the changes you suggest?

MICHAEL: It's 50/50 and I don't mind.

*   *   *

KEVIN: Would you be able to describe the effect you're seeking to have on your readers?

MICHAEL: Pleasure, in a word. Whatever I'm writing about, I think it's got to be a good experience, or not boring. You have to respect people's time. They haven't got time to read rubbish, and if they donate any time to you, you'd better make it worth their while.

KEVIN: Yes. And reading your poetry, I do get the feeling that you're, all the time, stretching yourself to give the best you can give.

MICHAEL: I think that's true; I'd hope so.

KEVIN: It brings a kind of intensity to even the funniest, wittiest of the poems.

MICHAEL: I like that compression. I'll leave a poem for years. There's a poem in *Another Fine Morning in Paradise*[7] that's thirty years old, for heaven's sake. I have them there in a folder, and I look at them every now and then and think, *You're bloody awful*. I'll go back and tweak it or I'll throw it out if it really frustrates me.

They're handwritten until I get them to a stage when I want a clean copy, and then I generally throw out all the previous bits. I know some people hang on to drafts as if they're gold, but I can't stand it. There are better poets whose drafts can teach me things. I've got books on Keats's craftsmanship, and others. I look at a poem and I think, *Gosh that was clever*, he seemed to have got it to a stage where it looked just right and then he's mucked around with it and changed bits again and I think, *Oh, that's instructive*.

Too many Australian poets hang on to drafts, and the poetry's not really worth hanging on to. That's a terrible thing to say, but I don't get it. Everyone, no matter what, can write a poem; everyone has a poem, but they're not all great poems; they can be fun poems for their friends or a sing-song or for a football game or a slogan. Not every poem's as good as Bushells, you know.[8]

I respect craftsmanship; the poets I like tend to be people who have this amazing sense of tact; it could be John Ashbery, it could be Billy Collins, it could be Alex Skovron.[9] People who seem to know when

111

enough is enough—or how to play with excess. Frederick Seidel is another one who's immensely good at occasionally going berserk, but then pulling back. He can say things that are totally outrageous and he does. He's got a line about 'Eating buttered toast in bed with cunty fingers on Sunday morning',[10] I thought this an amazing line, and then I found that he's stolen it from Henry Green, the English novelist.[11] I thought, that's clever of Seidel: he's lifting lines out of anywhere he can get them. It goes with the old expression, 'Good writers borrow, great writers steal'.[12]

KEVIN: You don't think there's some ethical question attached to that?

MICHAEL: I don't think so at all. It's a different sort of thing than plagiarising a whole poem. I like the idea of the cento; a poem that's made up of tags and scraps.

KEVIN: Which you're very good at. Let's move on. I'll just re-read that Auden quote, *When we genuinely speak we do not have the words ready to do our bidding, we have to find them, and we do not know exactly what we're going to say until we've said it and we say and hear something new that has never been said or heard before.* Do you have a response to that? And connected with that, what's your process in finding the words to fill your poems?

MICHAEL: To get an idea down, as it's happening. Quite often, I can't get to the end because I can't write as fast I can think of stuff. Or what you think is a great idea looks boring on paper, so you've got to wrestle with it. Sometimes it means re-writing the whole poem or reversing the order of things, switching things around: this line shouldn't be there, that's where it should start.

KEVIN: That, in a sense, that's the aftermath.

MICHAEL: It is, but it's also tied up with the first frustration of knowing, as you're writing it, that this isn't the precise word. Then you go back and start ransacking your mind or go for a walk or think, *I've got to look in a dictionary or a thesaurus.* That's where the word may appear;

or it may not at all. That's why sometimes I'll leave the draft. I've got stacks of the damn things. They're all poems *in utero*, they're not ready yet, they can't jump out into the world.

KEVIN: It sounds like what you're saying is you have an idea and you're seeking the words for it, rather than the words taking you to an idea.

MICHAEL: The words do take you to an idea to start with, but then the idea is not entirely formed. Sometimes you hear a pattern, a rhythm, or sound and language, all at once. Music and poetry are tied up for me. That sounds odd. I don't think of a tune and then match it. But there's this insistence, and you think, *that's a weird way of saying it*, and you write something down and think, *I wonder where that'll go?* So you take the pencil for a walk to find it.[13] Sometimes it falls out, and sometimes it won't. I don't know that I start with an idea, pure and simple, and find words to match it; that makes it sound too mechanical. It's a collision.

KEVIN: Do you take words from conversations?

MICHAEL: Of course, I love that. I love the story I heard on a train where someone's talking to an old mother who's partly gaga.

She says, *You'll like it when you get there, we've got some lovely geraniums outside.*

The mother says, *I don't like Germans, my husband fought them in the war.*

No dear, they're geraniums, they're outside the window.

I don't want any Germans coming in the window.

And I thought, this is getting zanier and zanier. That sort of stuff, I can't turn it into a poem because it's just a vignette, but that's the sort of thing you occasionally see and hear—the oddest things, graffiti or tags of conversation and especially the slang and general street talk of people.

KEVIN: It's easier to take what you find when you don't know the people. Are there limits to what you would take, what you find, when you know the people?

MICHAEL: No, I'd steal it from anyone.

KEVIN: I'll be more careful in future.

MICHAEL: Oh, yeah, I think of your poem about the poets stealing lines . . .

KEVIN: 'Thugs'.[14] "You're a thug."

MICHAEL: That's right. I think that you have to take what's available. For heaven's sake, I can't imagine Chaucer thinking, *Oh, I mustn't say that.*

* * *

KEVIN: Can you characterise the critical voice, or the critical voices, that you apply to your work? Is there a school of critical thought or are there particular critics or people in your network who you think are providing you with the stance, the critical stance toward your own work?

MICHAEL: Probably not immediately. There are people whose attitudes to poetry I like. I like to read lots of interviews with people. Some of the writings of folks like Jack Spicer[15] or William Carlos Williams—who are being pumped by an interviewer: *Why do you write like that?*—explaining *Is there any other way?* I'd like to think I have the confidence that some people have, of trusting entirely my own judgement, but I can't, so I fire work to people with a different range of attitudes.

KEVIN: What do you think of IA Richards' exercise in practical criticism where he typed out poems by famous poets and gave them to students to read and assess as if they were unpublished or student work?

114

MICHAEL: That's interesting, and I've done that sort of trick as well with people in workshops. I don't know that it's valid. At one stage I floated around a whole set of descriptions of water or coastal scenes that I'd taken from about 30-odd Australian poets, just lines here and there and stanzas. I asked people if there's anything here that strikes a bell, and *Who do you think's responsible for it?* There was only one person who spotted that it was a poem by someone she knew because it was her own.

I do think that the Richards thing is partly a bit of a have because anyone who's familiar with the whole canon, as they would have been back then, would have spotted certain signals as to the thought processes evident in the language and vocabulary and structure. One of the things that got me about that school of just reading poems cold and pretending nothing else exists: it couldn't happen if you were well read. You would always know that this is within so many years or months: it's got to be by George Herbert; it's got to be a John Donne—there's a turn of phrase, there's a field of allusion, of imagery, of vocabulary—as if you couldn't tell a Herrick from a Suckling.[16] I think that it's probably more difficult nowadays: if you float modern poems past people and say, *Who wrote it?*, they might say, *Oh gosh, I can hardly read it, it must be Michael Farrell's.* People will read a lot of stuff by their contemporaries, but I don't know if they're reading back, and further than the Anglosphere, so how many languages they have may be an interesting thing to explore.

KEVIN: How many languages do you work across?

MICHAEL: I don't work across many languages at all. I have a working knowledge of Latin, and Winifred and I occasionally will amuse ourselves by playing Scrabble with a Latin set. I can read serviceable French and serviceably tackle a bit of Italian, but I wouldn't say that I'm terrific at languages.

KEVIN: Focussing on composition: how important is mood, or does mood play a role for you?

MICHAEL: I think it probably does. It's the mood of the poem, or the mood of the poet. I think you angle for a certain thing. David Musgrave talks about tone, and he's really strong on that. I like to wrestle a poem into shape so that you end up with a mood at the end, even though it may be very slippery. I like that, what Byron called mobility.[17]

KEVIN: So do you need to be in a mood to write?

MICHAEL: Some sort of equilibrium, some sort of a freedom from other preoccupations. I think it's best to let it come when it comes and be ready for it, so to speak. It's not as if the muse is yelling out, *Hey catch this*, but there's a sense in which you can be tied up with things.

KEVIN: And when you're writing how quickly do you write?

MICHAEL: Pretty quickly. I like to get as much down as I can until it's run into slop, it just sort of dies somewhere, and then I'll come back and have a look at it, possibly a lot later.

KEVIN: When you are in a writing session, what brings that to a halt? Also, when you're working on a poem, and re-working and re-working it, what brings that to a halt, eventually?

MICHAEL: Well the first one's probably something like disgust at how bad it is. It's not going, it's not happening, you think, *I've got to stop here because I've pushed it beyond what's useful or practicable and it's not going to work at this stage*. I've got to go back a bit and come at it again. I think very few poems I write get done in one go, I can't think of any for yonks, unless they're very small and very tight. But then, I'm deliberately aiming for longer poems at the moment. It makes it hard too because there's not many places that publish longer poems.

KEVIN: Although there's a few prizes for longer poems, these days.

MICHAEL: Yes there are, but I don't always have a poem ready for it. I don't consciously aim to write one that will fit. I admire people who do.

KEVIN: So coming back to finishing, how do you know that a poem is finished? Or how does that experience arrive?

MICHAEL: I think it's a sense where you can't add anything to it without spoiling it or without taking it in a totally new direction. I think *That's it*; it declares itself done. Quite often you've overwritten it anyway, and you go back and you think, *I didn't need that*, so you throw out a stanza or a line or whole group of things.

KEVIN: It was interesting to me doing my *New and Selected*[18] that sometimes some very old poems continued to have obvious flaws that I couldn't see, but John Leonard could see, pretty quickly, and when he pointed them out it was clear to me that, yeah, that part of that poem should just disappear.

MICHAEL: He's good like that. John looked at a lot of my stuff too. He wanted me to throw him a manuscript at one stage. He'd went through it saying, *Out of so many poems, I'll have this and this, but I don't like this, I don't want that.* I said, *I can see which way the book's shaping up; you've ended up with a book that reads too nicely and*—I couldn't think of another word, so I said, *It's comfortable, it's cosy, it's nice and I'm not interested in nice.*

KEVIN: Was that *The Sweeping Plain*? And was that a breakthrough book for you?

MICHAEL: Yes. It was, in a way. It was a clearing of the decks and getting away from other things. I was moving into a more coherent, cohesive sense of what I was doing. The later book, *Another Fine Morning in Paradise*, was as well. But the next one; it wants to be completely different, it wants to be poems that use the word *I* quite unabashedly.

KEVIN: One of the things I noticed about this book is the absence of *I*. This last time through it, I was very aware of that.

MICHAEL: I was too. I think in both those last two, there was a deliberate distancing. I can distance it even with using the word *I*, because

I can make the *I* into a character that's quite unbelievable. It's not the *me*, personal.

KEVIN: Is there anything your readers owe you?

MICHAEL: Just the kindness.

KEVIN: They owe you $24.95 per book?

MICHAEL: No, just the kindness of their attention.

NOTES

1   Poet Kit Kelen was one of the initiators of the year-long poetry/creative project 366 (365 days plus leap day) which involved participants contributing daily, or less regularly, a poem or image to a social media site. See http://366metablog.blogspot.co.uk/

2   Hawthorne, Nathaniel 1853 *Tanglewood Tales. A Wonder Book for Boys and Girls*, Boston: Ticknor, Reed and Fields

3   Roland Robinson (1912–1992) published several collections of poetry including the award-winning *Tumult of the Swans*, Edwards and Shaw, 1953

4   'Make it new' is both the title of a book of essays by the poet Ezra Pound (New Directions, 1968) and his famous challenge to modern poets

5   Shelley, Percy Bysshe 1842 *The Masque of Anarchy*, London: Watson

6   Boehm, Philip 2014 *The Art of Fiction* No. 225: Herta Müller, Paris Review 210: 133–63

7   Sharkey, Michael 2012 *Another Fine Morning in Paradise*, Parkville: Five Islands Press

8   'Is it as good as Bushells?' was a 1990s advertising slogan for a brand of teabags

9   John Ashbery (1927–2017), major US poet, and New York State Laureate 2001 to 2003; Billy Collins, US Poet Laureate 2001 to 2003, known for his witty poems which he describes as 'suburban' and 'domestic' (see http://www.powells.com/post/interviews/billy-collins-bringing-poetry-to-the-public); Alex Skovron, Melbourne-based editor and poet

10 Seidel, Frederick 2016 'Widening Income Inequality' from *Widening Income Inequality*, New York: Farrar, Straus and Giroux

11 Green, Henry 1945 *Loving*, London: Hogarth Press

12 TS Eliot's famous line: 'Immature poets imitate, mature poets steal'; from the essay 'Philip Massinger' in *The Sacred Wood: Essays on Poetry and Criticism*, London: Faber & Faber, 1928

13 Paul Klee's famous line about drawing as 'taking a line for a walk'; see his *Pedagogical Sketchbook* (trans Sibyl Moholy-Nagy), New York: Praeger, 1953

14 Brophy, Kevin 2002 'Advice to Poets' from *Portrait in Skin*, Parkville: Five Islands Press

15 Jack Spicer (1925–1965); US poet, part of the Berkeley Renaissance that later morphed into the San Francisco Renaissance

16 John Suckling (1609–1641), English poet of wit; Robert Herrick (1591–1674), English lyric poet

17 Lord Byron (1788–1824), explicitly used this term in Don Juan sIV: 'that vivacious versatility, / Which many people take for want of heart. / They err—'tis merely what is call'd mobility, / A thing of temperament—and not of art'; see Byron, George Gordon 'Don Juan' in Jerome J McGann (ed), *The Complete Poetical Works*, Oxford: Oxford University Press, 1986

18 Brophy, Kevin 2013 *Walking: New and Selected Poems*, Elwood: John Leonard Press

19 Sharkey, Michael 2007 *The Sweeping Plain*, Carlton: Five Islands Press

"You have to wrestle with it sometimes"
Mike Ladd

Adelaide, South Australia

MIKE: I grew up in a semi-rural urban fringe, at Blackwood in the Adelaide hills. Our house was on a dirt road, at the very edge of the suburbs, and the whole area was about to be colonised by further suburbs. Blackwood is now very suburban with traffic lights and bitumen, but back in those days there were paddocks all around and a creek at the bottom of the hill, which was our playground. We were free to wander. So from early on I had this sense of a natural world, but also of a natural world that was threatened or being encroached upon.

JEN: Were your parents concerned about development?

MIKE: We were part of it, weren't we? My father was a soil scientist so he was very tuned into natural cycles of the world. And my mum is a bit of a conservationist. They certainly gave me a respect for nature and for learning about it. I've always been interested in that border zone of the urban, the industrial and nature, and how nature survives in that environment. Vestiges and edges. It's not a classical, pristine nature that I was connected to. It was a nature that was a border zone, and under threat. I can remember that feeling from way back, and to me that has always been associated with poetry. My very first poems were connected to that feeling.

JEN: You weren't writing pastorals?

MIKE: No. But they were about that particular Blackwood landscape. As a child, I was also intrigued by uncles who could recite Paterson[1] and other nineteenth-century poets. The landscapes, rhythmic language and sound play were something I was immediately interested in.

JEN: So you were interested in a combination of rhythm and cadence and content, all in one.

MIKE: That's right. It was something I felt very sympathetic to, as a child. Before I was a teenager I would be hearing words in my head, some kind of music. And that's really what stayed with me. I still start a poem that way usually. Almost always it comes to me as a phrase, as a cadence. Maybe just a few bars, and then I go on with the process of exploring where that is going to take me. It's often triggered by something immediate in the environment that I hear or see. I don't know how it's going to finish. I don't know if what I heard was the beginning of the poem or the end of the poem. But usually, as I'm hearing that, I know it's time to write. That writing could happen anywhere. It could be on the bus. It could be in the library. It could be here in my study. It could be in bed. It's not planned. I'm a hand-to-mouth writer.

JEN: So it's not conscious then: you let the poetry come to you.

MIKE: I do. I don't often sit and think of something that happened to me twenty-five years ago, although just recently a lot of old memories have been coming back. I rarely try to write about a pre-chosen subject, though sometimes research will prompt a poem. Mostly it's unconscious. The conscious side happens when I write the next draft. I'm consciously editing; and that process is informed by the other part of my practice: I read lots of world poetry.

Almost all of my editing involves erasure. I've almost always written too much. It's rare that I've written too little.

JEN: So you pour stuff out on a page? Once it starts coming, it keeps coming.

MIKE: That's right. I usually know when it's finished. It just stops. It peters out. I go over it and almost always I'll think, *The poem doesn't start on that line, it starts three lines down.* Or, *I've run out of poetry here, this is where it stops, the rest doesn't need to be here.*

JEN: It's as though your brain gives you a surfeit of material, and your work is to pick out the right parts of that?

MIKE: Yes: to pick out the *true* bits. Sometimes that takes a long time. Occasionally I'll get a poem almost as if it's dictated, and it's had very few changes in it. That's always a great joy. Even so, my practice is to put it away for a while and then come back to it and see if I still think it's right. If I think it's okay, after a month or two of having it in the drawer, I will send it away somewhere. Part of my filtering process is that I send it to various magazines and journals to see if other editors think it's worth publishing. It's like making wine. You pick the grapes, crush it, make it. Then you put it down for a while and see if it's still good. Then you do some taste tests. If it passes that, then I put it in the folder for the next book. I might still reject it at the end because it doesn't fit with the next book.

JEN: Does the fact the publisher has accepted it mean you remain happy with it?

MIKE: Not necessarily. But over the years very few publishers have taken poems that I later wished were not published. On the other hand, many have done me a favour by rejecting poems that I later realised were no good, or not good enough yet.

JEN: So when you get a rejection, you look at it again and decide whether it is a problem with the poem or a problem with the timing?

MIKE: That's right. It's a conversation between the editors and you. Some editors give you concrete suggestions and it's up to you to act on them or not. Occasionally I've dropped a stanza or added a bit, based on that advice. Sometimes I've just tried the same poem elsewhere. It's surprising how often you will succeed with a second or third editor when the first one wasn't interested. Perhaps you'll tinker a bit more, but then you find someone whose ear is attuned to it. You also have to have faith in yourself; but I do like having that other ear, that other eye as part of that judgment process.

JEN: Is there anybody else you use for that process?

MIKE: I used to belong to writers' groups: I had a monthly writers' group called the *Hot Seat*, because each month someone was in the hot seat and you'd send your poems or prose out in advance. The other members were John Griffin, Barry Westburg, Peter Goldsworthy, Peter McFarlane.[2] Later I was in a group with Kate Llewellyn and Patricia Irvine. These were casual; we gave each other notes and feedback. I don't do that so much anymore.

JEN: Do you know why? Do you not need it?

MIKE: Maybe I don't need it. Or don't have the time. I'm under the pump with ABC and Literature Board work these days.[3] I'm also mentoring a couple of other poets and I enjoy that. Between all that I don't have so much time for an actual writers' group. I also think I've got better at seeing my own weaknesses.

JEN: Not so much the naïve eye any more, then?

MIKE: No. I started publishing poems when I was a teenager, in school magazines and a national anthology called *Youth Writes*. I also started reading very deeply, especially certain poets. I was given an edition of Robert Frost for my sixteenth birthday because I was always talking about him to my parents. I read that book very deeply. My grandfather was a closet poet. He'd written poems but never published any in his lifetime, but he had a good poetry collection.

JEN: Did you talk to him about poetry?

MIKE: No. Never. I was too young when he died. Later, I was starting to publish some poems and my grandmother thought, *Why don't we give Grandfather's books to Michael?* They're right here on the wall. These are all my grandfather's books. That was a rather nice inheritance.

Mainly English canon, but also some modern stuff up to Yevtushenko. Reading of a lot of poetry became part of my process. Going to Adelaide University, I studied modern American and Australian poetry. One of my tutors was Andrew Taylor, and through him I went to Friendly Street,[4] which was important for Adelaide poets.

JEN: It seems to have been a real seedbed in Adelaide.

MIKE: It was. It was important. It started the night the Whitlam government was sacked. I started reading there at the age of seventeen. Dreadful stuff mostly.

JEN: Bringing in dreadful adolescent poetry was a bold move, but it also shows you were interested in listening to other people, and finding out what else you could be doing.

MIKE: That's right. You learnt from listening to others. And in the early days the quality was generally high. Andrew Taylor, Kate Llewellyn, John Bray, Peter Goldsworthy, guest appearances from Mark Strand and Bruce Dawe. You also got instant feedback from the audience. There tended to be a silent reaction if it was a bad poem, and warm applause if it wasn't. And it was exciting. Sometimes there was heckling. That was another part of the process. It produced its own style. Some things are much better on a page than they are in a live reading. You had to be aware of that. Within three or four months I stopped bringing bad poems and I started bringing better poems. And I started getting some positive feedback from people. That was a big boost of confidence.

I sent a poem to Rodney Hall, the editor of *The Weekend Australian*, and got a four-page rejection letter back, saying *I don't think that's quite ready for the paper, but I think you have talent.* He gave me a lot of feedback on the poem. It's a wonderful letter, I've still got it. That was a big factor in thinking, *Actually maybe I can be a poet.* I tried again and didn't get in and then the third time I tried he said, *Yes, this one's ready for the paper.* That was a big boost.

JEN: You were still a kid then?

MIKE: I was seventeen. I started writing prolifically, too much. I was studying modernism, studying all these interesting poets. I was immersed in it, and pouring out three, four poems a week.

JEN: In your voice, or in the voice of modernism?

MIKE: You could tell the influences. You could hear Yeats in a phrase, Wallace Stevens in a phrase. Eliot from time to time. It's practising. You absorb all these voices and eventually your own comes out of it. I'm still tinkering with my own voice. People say they can recognise a Mike Ladd poem but I don't know about that. I don't have a good handle on that at all. I never think that I'm writing a Mike Ladd poem, I'm just writing the next one. And I'm trying to experiment too.

Through Friendly Street I got my first book published, *The Crack in the Crib*.[5] I finished university in 1979, and finished that first book by 1981. It didn't become real until 1984. At university I got involved in radio: I had a little radio show called Radioactive Poetry.

JEN: So you've been doing poetry and radio all your adult life?

MIKE: That's right. I've always seen poetry as not just a page phenomenon, but as something that goes beyond the page, and can go into other media like radio, audio, video, installation.

I got involved in bands after I left university. I was writing the lyrics for a punk new wave band called *The Lounge* and supposedly singing them, but I don't think I was ever a singer. It wasn't exactly singing. That was another branch of poetry for me. It was one of the most creative periods of my life. The band lived in a house in the inner industrial west of Adelaide and we survived on the dole and our earnings from playing live, so all day we focussed on writing and practising songs.

At the same time I started doing these things called drum poems. I was interested in industrialised sites. I was interested in their rhythms. I was recording the sounds of panel-beating factories and railway crossings, and working those into the poems.

JEN: And they came out of the industrial sites?

MIKE: Yes. I formed some ensembles with percussionists who would imitate those rhythms on found industrial materials, building drums out of 44-gallon drums and bits of industrial piping. It was exciting. We used to perform them at rock-and-roll venues, between acts, and sometimes get booed off the stage. We were fairly punky about it and didn't mind that.

At the same time I met my wife Cath, who was studying at art school.[6] We worked together with me reciting poems to her visual projections, and making short films, super eight films with poetic words in them. She has contributed artwork or photography to all my books and we have made public installations, putting poems on street signs and billboards. We're still involved with collaborations.

*   *   *

JEN: One of the questions we have is about what sustains you in your writing life.

MIKE: It's a really interesting question. From an early age I was encouraged, so I think one thing that sustains you is that other people like your work. I was always encouraged, and part of what sustains me is the knowledge that I might not have millions of readers, but I have had a lot of good feedback. Individuals who've said, *I love that poem*, or, *I cut your poem out of the newspaper and stuck it on my fridge*. Little things like that are enough to sustain me. And the occasional good review. Those things are important. I wonder, if I'd only had terrible reviews, whether I'd still be doing it. I don't know.

JEN: You might not be putting it out: you might be secretly writing, like your grandfather did.

MIKE: Exactly. I might just write it and hide it. It might just go into the drawer.

JEN: So there's a lot of drive that keeps you writing?

MIKE: It's an inner drive. I'm always listening for that voice, the initiator of a poem. What sustains me is the desire itself. If that is not satisfied I'm somehow frustrated. I feel like I'm not doing something that I should be doing to make myself complete.

The company of other poets sustains me. I was a regular at the Lee Marvin reading, which was the one Ken Bolton coordinated for many years. I found that a conducive and stimulating reading. Ken has retired from that now, but there is still the Halifax café reading run by Jelena Dinic and Ian Gibbins. I think that's the best poetry reading in Adelaide at the moment.

Poetica sustained me even though it drained me as well, because I was always working on other people's stuff. A large amount of energy went into other people's writing. Producing it and making it sound good and interesting on the radio. At the same time though, I was digging down, I was meeting poets from all around the world, and getting to know what makes them tick.

JEN: You've probably had more exposure to poets than most other people in the country.

MIKE: It gave me a lot of inside knowledge, and also stimulus. Sometimes I've beaten myself up about not dedicating myself to my own writing full time and what I could have produced if I had, but then I realise my radio work is another kind of writing. It's writing with a microphone as well as a pen. And when I look at it that way, I have made my living as a writer for thirty-five years now.

Another thing that sustains me is travel. Poetry hasn't given me a lot of money, but it has given me a lot of travel and friends. Whenever I travel I take a big diary with me. This is my South American diary. I fill it up with poems and ideas.

Walking often produces poetry in me. This book, *Karrawirra Parri*—
which was a haibun— was a poet's journey, which involved walking
the River Torrens from source to sea.[7] The process of a walking journey
stimulated me to write. I won a Barbara Hanrahan fellowship that
allowed me to take time off, so I had the freedom each day to be out
in a mostly natural environment, but again with some industrial elements impinging on it. The footsteps produce words as well as miles,
you know; there's actually something in that physicality of walking.

JEN: Rousseau wrote a whole book on walking and writing.[8]

MIKE: Many of my favourite poets were great walkers: Wordsworth,
Mandelstam, Basho. That was a rare case of deliberately choosing a
journey and seeing if that would produce writing, as opposed to waiting for words to come.

JEN: Do you remember when you first came across a poem? When
you actually saw something that you knew was a poem?

MIKE: I was going to say it would go back to chants and songs, so I
didn't *see* it first, I *heard* it. I have a very early memory of my grandmother bathing me and singing the chant 'Swim Sam swim, swim
across the dam'. My grandfather was a fan of Masefield and I remember him reciting, *I must go down to the seas again, to the lonely sea and
the sky.*[9] I was six or seven years old. And I remember thinking, That's
not normal speech, that's something different. That's a poem. That's
word music.

JEN: At school, did you have good teachers? Were they supportive of
poetry?

MIKE: I had a good first year high school English teacher called Don
Pike. He taught me irony too. His favourite stuff was ironic writing,
more in prose than poetry. But he taught me the idea of irony. In high
school we did people like Wilfred Owen, and I still love Owen. I got
interested in breakaways from that, through Frost and then Eliot. And

then Ginsberg. I started to break out of the traditional English mode and discover the Americans when I was sixteen or seventeen.

JEN: That seems to have been quite a big thing for Australian poets: it seems you didn't get much exposure to the Americans until later, and then everybody seems to have been tremendously moved by them.

MIKE: Yes, there was that influential anthology *Contemporary American and Australian Poetry* edited by Tom Shapcott, that had an impact on me in the late seventies. There was also the generation before me, the generation of 1968, like Tranter and Adamson.[10] They were about getting rid of the heavy English influence on Australian poetry and embracing the Americans, particularly the New York school and some of the Californians. But for me, coming along later, the English didn't just mean Auden and Larkin; it meant Linton Kwesi Johnson and the Mersey poets, and I liked them! As for the Americans, I liked O'Hara a lot, but thought Ashbery was a drag. Same with Olsen. At the time I was more into Whitman and Wallace Stevens and then Garry Snyder, the Beats, Galway Kinnell. Plus there was a whole world of poetry in translation to consider: Basho, Hikmet, Szymborska, Popa.[11]

After the American expansiveness, I got excited by European minimalism. For my second book, *Picture's Edge*,[12] I worked with Miroslav Holub.[13] He'd been brought out to the Adelaide Festival Writers' Week. Arts SA paid him to stay on to do workshops with four or five local poets. I applied and was lucky enough to get in. Holub helped me with the book and part of it is his influence. These are all spare, small poems, very minimalist. I was very keen on him. I'm not sure how we got here, but anyway. Where were we going?

JEN: We started with encountering poetry and then moved on to that ocean of American poetry and the modern European poets.

MIKE: Yes. I had that tension between the two. I'm still resolving that, really. You write between those sorts of tensions, don't you? You're really a whole soup of influences, and we shouldn't forget Australian influences either. Early on for me it was Dransfield, then Peter Goldsworthy and Kate Llewellyn, Dorothy Hewett, Forbes, Murray. I've never felt I belonged to any school though.

JEN: Would you call yourself a South Australian poet? Would you call yourself a modernist poet or something else?

MIKE: No. I don't. Kinsella called me a poetic loner. [14]

JEN: Would you call yourself a poet? If you met somebody for the first time would you introduce yourself as a poet?

MIKE: These days I often just call myself a writer because I'm writing a lot of prose as well. *Karrawirra Parri* was half prose, half poetry. And my most recent book is eight prose pieces and 30 poems, which relate to each other. It's called *Invisible Mending*,[15] and it's about how the world both scars us and heals us. A lot of the prose is not fiction, it's creative nonfiction. But to get back to your question: I would tend to call myself a writer. In 2006 I was invited to the Venezuelan International Poetry Festival, and I did write on my application to enter the country, *poet*. It felt really good. In the past I've often put *radio producer*. I rocked up in Caracas airport and there was a border guard, a lovely dark-haired woman with a hat, and with epaulettes. She looked at my application and said, *Poeta, you are welcome to my country*.

It did feel good to call myself a poet. But because I write radio scripts, I write prose, I write reviews and articles, I like the term *writer*. It's got a humbleness to it, like I'm a jack-of-all-trades, which I probably am.

JEN: Most writers are jacks-of-all-trades. They can't usually make a living from one form. Do you see your poetry writing as a way to engage with social/political things that disturb you?

MIKE: Yes, I do. I don't think that it's often overt. There have been some. I wrote a poem, back in the previous John Howard regime, called the 'Immigration Minister's Dream' about our brutal border policies.[16] I've also written about such things as the Iraq war, and the ongoing question of the European theft of Australia from its Indigenous people. You have to be careful as a writer not to get too tract-like, but there are times when it's necessary to stand up and be counted. One of my biggest political commitments is to the environment, and I'm not partisan. I've got lots of beefs with both major parties on that. There are metaphors in my work that are political in that sense.

In the *Invisible Mending* book, there's a poem called 'Reveg'. It's about planting little native cypress trees on a denuded hill that was once a sheep station. It talks about the hill having a concentration camp haircut, as though it is a prisoner, and the last line is, 'it is growing two hundred years of our madness out'.

*   *   *

JEN: Let's move to the writing sector, and its connection to your work, and here I mean everything from publishers to agents to bookstores. How much do you rely on them? How much do you think about that as being part of the world you're in?

MIKE: I've never had an agent, but I rely on my publishers to help me connect with readers. I try and publish new work all over the place including obscure journals and websites and I generally say yes to invitations to read, even in very small bookshops.

JEN: Why 'all over the place'? Is that to build a broader reading?

MIKE: Yes. You get a sense of people who like your work and who are going to publish it. I tend to target places where I know they'll probably like it. It's mostly in Australia, but I do a bit overseas as well.

The book publishing sector is small for poetry, so you tend to know who the editors are. They can't look at too many books because they've already got a stable and a backlog, and they're trying to shift what they've got, so it's pretty tight. A couple of times a year I would be asked to a festival. I enjoy that side of it. Running the Radio National poetry show was another side to it.

JEN: So you were actually part of the publishing sector.

MIKE: Yes. If you look at the number of listeners *Poetica* had, we were the biggest poetry publisher in the country, with 70,000 listeners every week. There were several reasons for it. Firstly, it was because we were on a network that has a large loyal audience. But there was also the factor that not everyone was listening for poetry; it was just that it came on, on their favourite station, and straight into their lounge room. If they liked it they stayed with it, even if they were not into poetry as such. So it was the access. We were reaching more than the usual poetry suspects. You didn't have to go out and find this little hole-in-the-wall poetry reading and sit down in a chair and listen.

It was also carefully curated to appeal to both the poetry specialist and the average Radio National punter. And I'd like to put on record that we had an excellent team of producers from the now defunct ABC Radio Drama department who made the show. I was the editor but I had a lot of support in making the programs. I chose the poetry carefully. Some stuff might be very good poetry, but it needs to be studied on a page or read many times. That does not work on radio, because people have to hear it, they're not reading it. They have to hear it and get something out of it. So I tended to choose the more concrete, the more image-rich, the more narrative, the more story-telling poems that would hold an audience. We actually had to hold an audience to survive; and we did manage that for seventeen years.

The third factor is that radio is a lovely medium for poetry. It's that word-music thing again. If you get a good poet who can read their work well, it's a wonderful experience. And there's nothing between you and the reading, with radio. It's just straight into your mind. You don't have to use your eyes, your hand; you can be doing something else. You can be driving your car, or painting. With television, they've got to decide what they're going to show you. Radio, given it is an oral and an aural medium, is ideal for poetry. Red Room are currently doing some interesting podcasts,[17] but it's a shame there is so little poetry broadcast on the ABC now. At least a lot of the old *Poetica*s are still available online as podcasts.

When *Poetica* was axed in 2015, I became quite depressed. I had hoped to do it for a few more years then hand it over as a going concern to a new generation, but that dream was shattered. There was no obvious reason to cut it. Our audience was still strong even though the management mucked around with our timeslot and presenters. It was dumped because the Abbott government pulled $250 million from the ABC, and there were a whole lot of good programs that died from lack of funding, but really the ABC management could have looked at other areas to cut, and sadly I'd have to say that the people who are running the ABC these days are not so much into the old cultural values of public broadcasting, but are more pseudo-commercial in their approach. These days I make documentaries for Radio National, mainly about Australian history, but I still get to weave in a bit of poetry from time to time.

* * *

JEN: In the questions I sent you, there was that Auden quote from *Secondary Worlds,* his TS Eliot memorial lectures. He said, *When we genuinely speak we don't have the words ready to do our bidding. We have to find them and we don't know exactly what we're going to say until we've said it. And we say and hear something new that's never been said or heard before*. Does that strike any bells with you?

MIKE: Well, I think it chimes with what I said in the very beginning about how I hear a phrase, that's the start of the poem and I don't know where it's going to take me until I get there. You have to follow it and you have to wrestle with it sometimes too. You have to wrestle with the editing as to whether you've been true to it or not, or whether it's worth something or not to you.

JEN: Do you have that same experience with prose?

MIKE: Yes. Not as much though. Poetry is far more demanding and meticulous for me. Poetry is hard on the brain. You have to compose its every syllable. I'm looser in prose. I still like to polish it, but I'm more freewheeling, whereas the poetry is a demanding task master. Every syllable has to be right.

To go back to Auden, at the end you want to know what it is saying. You want to ask yourself, *What am I saying*? But you don't have to know that at the beginning. Even during the editing phase, you might play with the structure and the sound and still ask, *What am I actually saying*?

JEN: Yes. You need to know before you can let it go. The words come to you first. Then, you said you sit and write, quite consciously following that line. And then you edit. Are you thinking and feeling differently when you're editing than when you're writing?

MIKE: I'm much more hard-nosed and clinical when I'm editing. I think I'm more carried away with the feeling with the first time. Let it just flow, and try and push it to see where it goes. The editing phase is much more *right, wrong*; that's in, that's out.

JEN: How do you recognise that moment of completion? How do you find it?

MIKE: Oh, that's hard. You're not 100 per cent correct of course. Look at an example like Robert Gray who is still tinkering with his collected poems, including things he published long ago.[18] He gave me the example of Bonnard who was on his deathbed, practically, still retouching his paintings. Or sneaking into museums and having his friend watch for the guard while he changed something. The short answer is: it's finished when I don't think I can do any better, and I think that's as good as I can make it. You eventually have to come to that point. And the other thing is that your energy has moved elsewhere and there's another one to do. That bird is as fledged as it's going to be.

JEN: Go out and fly, my pretty.

MIKE: And let the world decide if it's any good or not now. You can be responsible for it up to a certain point and then it's up to others. In the end it's out of your hands.

JEN: What sort of effect do you hope to have on your readers?

MIKE: This sounds terribly pretentious, but I hope to make them enjoy their lives a bit more at that point. I hope to offer an insight, an experience, that makes the day a bit more enjoyable or interesting.

I want them to actually enjoy the moment of the poem. It's not a didactic thing but I'm hopeful of passing on something. Why would I do that? I suppose that's the kind of guy I am. When I see a beautiful sight, or a bird, I point it out to my friend.

And I would say I am trying to please myself as a reader. I'm my first reader. When you write you're immediately split in two. Suddenly there's someone else sitting next to you at your writing desk; and that is you as a reader. You need to satisfy yourself. You need to know that is a good poem, or that is true, or feel enlightened.

JEN: So the 'you' sitting next to you is actually a critical reader, a critical voice?

MIKE: It is. And that's the person who does the draft. That's the person I'm trying to please first. And they're my toughest critic.

JEN: Is that critical-you carrying the critical voices of the great poets and critics from the past?

MIKE: I'm trying to live up to a standard. You know you're not getting there most of the time. You have to be careful who you compare yourself to otherwise you'd never pick up a pen again. I don't compare myself to Shakespeare otherwise I wouldn't do anything. Give yourself a break. Compare yourself to one of your contemporaries if you must. Internalise that great world of literature, the standard that you'd like to get to. That's important. Somebody could be an outsider poet, a naïve artist, and write fantastic stuff without it, but that's rare.

JEN: There's one last question; is there anything your readers owe you?

MIKE: Oh, gee, that's a tough one. No, they don't owe me much at all. Just the chance to prove myself again. And just common civility. That's all. If anything, I owe them, because I'm asking for their time and attention.

NOTES

1   Banjo Paterson (1864–1941), a journalist and bush poet, extensively published in *The Bulletin*. Perhaps most famously the author of 'Waltzing Matilda', he was a proponent of the bush ballad and presented romantic views of Australian rural life

2   John Griffin, poet and playwright; Barry Westburg, poet and academic; Peter Goldsworthy, poet, novelist and medical practitioner; Peter McFarlane, poet, writer and educator; Kate Llewellyn, poet, author and travel writer; Patricia Irvine, South Australian poet

3   The Literature Board of the Australia Council for the Arts

4   Friendly Street Poets is both a reading group and a publisher, based in Adelaide and established in 1976 by poets Andrew Taylor (poet and academic), Richard Tipping (sculpture and word artist known for his concrete poetry), and Ian Reid (poet, prose writer and editor). Friendly Street has supported careers and hosted readers for a surprising number of Australian poets, and continues to offer mentorship and opportunities to local poets

5   Ladd, Michael 1984 *The Crack in the Crib*, Unley: Friendly Street Poets

6   Cathy Brooks, multidisciplinary artist, involved also in community and urban arts projects

7   Ladd, Michael 2012 *Karrawirra Parri: Walking the Torrens from Source to Sea*, Kent Town: Wakefield Press

8   Rousseau, Jean-Jacques 2011 [1782] *Reveries of the Solitary Walker*. Trans. Russell Goulbourne Oxford: Oxford University Press

9   Masefield, John 1916 'Sea Fever' in *Salt-Water Poems and Ballads*, New York: Macmillan

10   John Tranter, Australian poet, editor and publisher; Robert Adamson, poet and publisher

11 Linton Kwesi Johnson: a Jamaica-born, UK-raised poet, who said of his work that 'Writing was a political act and poetry was a cultural weapon' (see 'I did my own thing: interview with Nicholas Wroe', *The Guardian*, 8 March 2008). The Mersey poets: typically listed as Roger McGough, Brian Patten and Adrian Henri, who were collected in the 1967 Penguin Modern Poets anthology *The Mersey Sound*. The Americans: Frank O'Hara (of the New York School); John Ashbery (often considered the major American voice); John Olson (well known for his prose poetry); the Beats, who were a product of 1950s San Francisco counterculture, and include Alan Ginsberg, Lawrence Ferlinghetti and Garry Snyder; and Galway Kinnell, whose poetry explores social, spiritual and environmental issues. Poets in translation: Matsuo Basho, master poet of the Edo period in Japan; Nazim Hikmet, known as the first modern Turkish poet; Wisława Szymborska, a Polish poet who won the Nobel prize in 1996; and Vasko Popa, Serbian modernist poet

12 Ladd, Michael 1994 *Picture's Edge*, Kent Town: Friendly Street Poets & Wakefield Press

13 A Czech poet and immunologist, Miroslav Holub (1923–1998) published his first collection of poetry in 1958, and came to Anglophone readers' attention in 1967 when Penguin published his *Selected Poems* in their series on modern European poets

14 John Kinsella, Australian poet, and editor of *Salt* journal; based in Western Australia

15 Ladd, Michael 2016 *Invisible Mending*, Mile End: Wakefield Press

16 Ladd, Michael 2005 'Immigration Minister's Dream', *Agenda* 41.1–2: 97–99

17 Red Room Poetry hosts its podcasts at https://www.stitcher.com/podcast/red-room-poetry-podcast

18 Robert Gray, poet and writer, based in New South Wales

"It's poetry itself that matters"
Philip Salom

Melbourne, Victoria

KEVIN: Let's assume that poets are connected to the world, and have a context around them. What are your points of connection to the world?

PHILIP: Before I was published, I had no supportive connection. In a funny kind of way this still applies to me. Most poets are *poets* before they are published poets; from early years they've wanted to *be a poet* as a vocation, they were teenage poets in the making, and therefore they were always in some sense connected. They were hoping they would succeed, or continue becoming more published, more practiced, more proficient characters in poetry. But my background was rural: farming, then Agricultural Science. I didn't know anything about literature; I didn't read any literature until I was 19 or so.

When I first discovered poetry it was by chance. I did creative writing and literature at university because I knew very little about either, but I had become interested in writing fiction. I met some older poets who were keen about poetry but they saw themselves as the *only* practitioners of it; anyone new, like myself, was considered to be one of their little admirers. That sort of role doesn't fit easily with me. I admire people, professionally, according to their merit. Even after my first few published books I knew these people were reluctant to accept me as a poet.

The first poet I met and who taught me, in Western Australia, said *You'll never be a poet, you're a scientist. All your background is scientific, you think like a scientist. You couldn't possibly be a poet.* This happened first when I was a student but he continued saying it *after* my first book was published and after it had been successful and won an international prize.[1]

So I learnt early on not to take too much notice of people who called themselves poets. It's poetry itself that matters. I'm far from a purist but I thought it was the poetry itself that mattered, not my personality, not their groups, not their assumptions about themselves, not their sense of history. I'm still pretty much like that.

After publishing several books I began to teach. I became involved with students and in those days in Western Australia that was a close association. We used to socialise and we'd have parties. I'd organise meals, we'd have gatherings, we all felt very much of a kind. I liked it. It's not done so much now, and it wasn't a matter of bed-hopping, it was a matter of a collective interest. There wasn't much alternative at the time; it just became a poetry scene.

Also I ran live poetry readings and a lot of those same people were involved. There were many other poets who had no interest in us, but would be quite happy to come along as guest readers. And I, being the impure person I am, would invite people whose poetry I didn't like but I knew had a standing of sorts, because I thought if you run a reading it's not just about your own poetics and your own crowd, it's about the larger thing.

That has always been my principle: poetry, and art forms as the larger dimension, are what really matter. So my connection, therefore, has been with books, with poetry itself and with individual poets I've met along the way. Now that I don't teach any more this immediacy of contact and connection has fallen away.

KEVIN: What difference has it made?

PHILIP: I'm not a person who has lots of friends. Alone-ness is an essential condition for my working life. I don't mind the isolation from that point of view. I well and truly live in my cave. Involvement with poetry is my own writing and reading. I've got one or two people I talk to, on and off, about poetry and other things but I don't like talking about poetry all the time; it's boring *all* the time.

KEVIN: What has sustained you in your writing life?

PHILIP: I have a straightforward answer to this: alcohol and domesticity; opposites in some way. And I mean it, I have enjoyed drinking most of my writing life. These two things sustain the self that is left over from the creative self.

KEVIN: Do you drink while you write?

PHILIP: No, not significantly, but I drink around it and I drink regularly and I sometimes drink a lot, probably more than I should for my health, but I enjoy it. It provides that other side of personality and relaxation. And altered-ness, of course. Writing is intense and done in some 'elsewhere', not domestic, not describable, not here. Away from writing I prefer to do something sensory, oral. I like eating, too.

Domesticity is the main other part of it, and the larger part. My main writing life overlapped with two marriages (one at a time) where I spent most of my life at home. I'm quite happy to do that, I'm a home-body in lots of ways. I might not have sustained a career if I'd been emotionally at a loose end or had a fraught emotional life. Perhaps I maintained a fairly stable emotional family life because it suits me. It gives me a controlled environment so the risks I take are in the work itself.

My ordinary self is sustained in those two ordinary ways, but how I sustain my creative-working self is far more profound: I live in hope of the next creative breakthrough into a body of work. I feel there is a very substantial work just out of knowing, apprehended, felt, out of reach now, but reachable. It's a work I have not yet created, maybe not yet earned, a work which will break new ground if I stay focused on the waiting. It will be a significant work. Paradoxically, one of the drives behind this expectation is doubt regarding the value of anything I have done in the past and this self-doubt is the grit I seem to take on in order to resist and therefore grow from, rather pearly and clichéd, I'm afraid—but true. I am not given to self-congratulation.

But I'm always, maybe foolishly, optimistic the next work might be a huge leap into the major chord. This is how I have felt about past work, and then it has come to me, been written, published, and had its (literal) day. It may not have struck others as significant; it may, it may become so; but it came through powerfully to me. It's for history to judge. I'm onto the next waiting.

KEVIN: Can you remember your first encounter with poetry? You talked a little bit about your early university encounter; were there any earlier than that?

PHILIP: At primary school, bush ballads. Which I now don't consider poetry. They're a verse form related to poetry. We could put them in with poetry but *I* don't call them poetry. They don't have the essentials—*the inner life* of poetry. They were actually more about myths of Australian-ness than poetry. That's why they were taught and that's how I understood them.

At high school, a couple of lyric poems were studied in English classes and I decided this was all very strange and foreign and I didn't want anything to do with it. I spent most of my English classes wagging it, in other words not at school. But then I spent a lot of time at school not at school, elsewhere, lots of elsewhere time. So poetry didn't become real and understood until I was in my twenties.

KEVIN: And was it a particular teacher or particular books?

PHILIP: I encountered Patrick White when I was living in the country; someone gave me *The Vivisector*[2] to read and, though I wouldn't have thought so at the time, it's a powerfully poetic kind of prose writing. The metaphoric power and the inner poetry is there, in small and large scale, in linguistic and thematic manner.

I never encountered lyric poetry until I was sharing a house with a Dylan Thomas fan, always reading Thomas. I acquired a record of Thomas being read by Richard Burton[3]—I swapped a Bob Dylan record (this will worry the purists of one kind for the purists of another)—I swapped a Bob Dylan record for *Under Milk Wood.* I'd listen to this extraordinary radio-play with Dylan Thomas poems my flatmate had. But I still wasn't interested in *writing* poetry. That came later.

I started to write prose and went to university (for the second time). I encountered people in the creative writing school, teaching poetry. There was one poet in particular who too often taught his own work, he intended to teach *himself* to first years. I think that's off in the extreme.

KEVIN: Yeah, I do, too. How much poetry do you read now?

PHILIP: I used to read a great deal of British and American poetry, and poetry in translation from Europe. And then I read for teaching because I was creating courses. I have bursts when I read a lot and then read little. Now, I tend to read haphazardly. I read less actual poetry and more for 'material'. I read nonfiction, neurology, psychoanalysis, mysticism, spiritual things. I read for the insights of the work. I don't just read for pure pleasure—or in poetry alone. I read for change. And I read for challenge and I read to keep my mind working. I'm interested in the way people conceptualise the world and particularly the way we make assumptions—how foolish we are. I think that all creative thinking can be, perhaps foolishly unexpected in order to cut through foolishness (Blake's 'persisting in folly'). Whereas there are some poets who write lyrical poetry which is just full of bullshit. I mean, I read their work and think *that's dishonest, it doesn't convince.* I am interested in ontological exploration but to me that requires rigour and honesty. And it's funny, finding poets whose work is for their personal charisma . . .

KEVIN: When you introduce yourself to strangers, do you identify yourself as a poet?

PHILIP: I had written my third book[4] before I ever said I was a poet to anyone other than people who already knew; so to strangers, no.

KEVIN: Now?

PHILIP: I'm more likely to, but not straight away. If you meet people for long enough and are talking they will end up asking questions where you may have to fudge it; you have to do what Auden used to do and say something else—a paleontologist or whatever it was he said—but then he was referring to complete strangers and there was no sustained conversation. He did it to avoid that.

I used not to say it when I was younger because I thought I hadn't earned the right, and that's where I am being purist. I thought I might not be a poet, I have written two books,[5] but I still might not be a poet, and I held some reserve. I held substantial value on the term 'poet'.

KEVIN: And would you add a descriptor to the kind of poet you are?

PHILIP: I hate that term—what *kind* of poet I am. I can't answer that question without a sense of vacuum. What are genre and form, and how to answer 'kind' without referring to these? It's like a spiritual question. One of the spiritual areas of insight that has interested me since my twenties has been Sufism. Sufism is full of such quandaries, starting with, *What is Sufism? What is spiritual understanding?* We can't answer the question because there's often no way the person asking the question can understand any kind of answer. Or even, to be honest, *want* to. The asking is merely automatic. A courtesy.

KEVIN: What about engagement with social and political issues? Does poetry offer you a way in to that?

PHILIP: Yes, it always has. One of the things I had in the back of my mind as a driving force, other than the desire to succeed at writing poetry, was a sense of framing injustice. The things that went wrong, the things that we did wrong, ran through as a theme. We are extremely flawed beings and when we institutionalise our being and pluralise it, we institutionalise injustice as much as any kind of justice. We say justice but we often create injustice.

I find that people in groups where any kind of power, any kind of decision making, is involved inevitably annoy me. In fact, I find all such gatherings faintly abhorrent and I see people doing all the things I don't like about people and the outcomes being the results of that behaviour. And so, injustices of all kinds. The world is unjust. We live in a world of accident and we live in a world of power and therefore we live in a world of fear and failing and there's no way around that.

KEVIN: I remember Doris Lessing asking the question in her autobiography,[6] *whoever told anybody that it was reasonable to expect fairness?*

PHILIP: Yeah, but it sits at the core of ethics, morality, religions. Most people are brought up to expect justice and to be given a fair deal without it being stated. In childhood, there's a lot that's unfair, that's fair, right and wrong. I realised as soon as I had a son how much children come ready for justice. Reading the first stories to a little kid who can just speak you find they are aware of injustice in the stories and you haven't said anything about it. They say, *That shouldn't have happened.* You think, *hang on, they're not abstract thinkers.* They feel it; it's an emotional reaction. Children *feel* injustice before they can frame it intellectually or abstractly, and that's extraordinary. My work has always had discovery contrasted with the daily and the social and the political—as a critique of some kind.

KEVIN: Well, the last three books, in particular.

PHILIP: *The Keepers Trilogy* is overtly satirical.[7] My novels *Waiting* and *Playback* could be called that, too.[8] Critique has always been present but being critical, including an element of the lightly farcical, say, in

Playback and the satirical, in *Waiting*. In other words, if you think about it there's a kind of strange wit about the conceptions that I've increasingly made, in poetry and prose. I am creating structures which are for that purpose, even though that's not their only purpose.

KEVIN: Let's talk about what part is played in your own poetic practise by your relationships to other poets. Did you have poet friends when you were first starting out, and is it important to you to feel that you work in a community of poets?

PHILIP: Oh, of course. I've written an essay on William HartSmith for the *Australian Poetry Journal*.[9] I mention Bill's comments about my early student work where he said, in my second year of study, *You are a poet.* That was said within a year of that other poet saying to me *you're not.* And I believed Bill whereas I didn't believe the other person. In my essay I say what matters about a strong poet is the way they call you to question your own work. The earlier rejection of my work was for some years driving me forward to be a poet, not backward. But I probably needed Bill's opinion to resist the rejection.

I have enough poets as friends now. Yes, I have, a few. A community of poets? No, I prefer close and intense poetry relationships rather than the larger. I have never felt truly part of a community. But I'm not a community minded person. I don't join in, I'm not a joiner. I'm very much a non-joiner.

KEVIN: You do go to quite a number of poetry events.

PHILIP: I do; I go to a lot. I go out of principle and when I know no one knows who I am. It's not even necessarily very pleasant going.

KEVIN: But why do you go then?

PHILIP: On principle. I think poetry should be supported. I've always believed that, even when I was of no consequence and now that I'm of a bit more consequence. I've been to poetry events where no poets have turned up. I've been to readings by poets who are really good, where no poets have turned up. Occasionally, it's happened to me. It's wrong. I really do think it's an injustice.

KEVIN: The writing sector, the publishers, agents—do they play a large part, for you?

PHILIP: Agents, no. Most small publishers have unpaid readers and I became one of them. I had occasionally read for the National Book Council when it existed, reading manuscripts for assessment. I've also written long reports on both academic work and reports for publishers. I've written work on behalf of poets for publishers and on behalf of publishers for poets. I've written reports for funding bodies, as we all do.

These are the hidden duties, unpaid duties; once again, it's what you give back. It is important; and it's different from networking, which I'm hopeless at, have no taste for. This service of reading and supporting is usually one-directional. You don't benefit from it personally. Obviously I strongly believe we should give back; I have little time for people who don't do any of this. I mean maybe their *work* is a giving, but a lot of people made huge gains and still do not give back and I think that's just shit, quite frankly. Surprisingly many people take the gains, the spoils, without question, in that way.

*   *   *

KEVIN: Is there anyone who reads and comments on your drafts now?

PHILIP: Not much, no. There never has been. I usually befriend my editors to find a closeness with them. I tell editors to say exactly what they want and be as straightforward as they can, short of making decisions. And I don't get upset, I take everything they say seriously. A critical balance is achieved. I take reviews seriously, too.

KEVIN: When you think about the effects you want to have on your readers, are you able to describe them?

PHILIP: Essentially I want my style and imagination, the feelings and ideas intrinsic to each work, to come alive in the reader's mind. And body. My work's impure, it mixes registers, is light and serious, uses metaphor as material and medium at times, is world-imagining and cross-associative, is conceptual in essence with sensory flesh. And it keeps changing, it's mercurial and inclined to re-invention. I ask a lot, but it's what I ask of myself as a reader. To be responsive. To let the work get inside and change me. I assume we are all pretty much hoping for that.

I hope people read the work closely, read it all the way through, or at least a poem or two or three or half a dozen in a book, read them closely and stop and think about what might be going on, and maybe read them closely again. I would hope my work has that effect and that's nothing to do with me. That's a principle that *precedes* my work; in other words, an abiding principle, that people should just give work that amount of credit to begin with.

Many people encounter a personality; they hear and read poetry as a spoken form because they hear the voice in it, they are searching for the voice, they are looking for the person in it. Many people never get past that. They want to like *the person* reading to them, before their poetry, and they want vulnerability, another aspect of that innocence I mentioned. Readers, audiences, want to be charmed, they want to be moved. I think they like poets to be a little weak, almost; lacking confidence so they can take them in. But powerfully weak! There's a lot of mothering, a compassion that is a power game that no one acknowledges in live performance. On the other side is the assumption that someone performing already has the status and they overwhelm the audience with charisma, not necessarily with poetry but their manner, with the poetry as a component. Irish accents work, too! Either way, there's a lot of posing.

I hope that my *poetry* can survive on its own merits even if those merits are not necessarily 'easy' ones. I hope people can read the larger themes, the abstractions, the length, and that they can perceive the conceptual underpinnings and the emotional underpinnings and the strange wit and enjoy the inventiveness of it, as well as the insight. I do think my work's inventive, I do think it's insightful.

KEVIN: I do too.

PHILIP: I hear it can be difficult to read. There is far more obscure work out there than mine, so it may be something more of the above than of linguistic complexity. I don't know. To be honest it frustrates me that people rarely say why. We should work our own style but also speak about what other poets' poetics might be. And in this I am a purist—getting back to that concept again. I will not qualify my work or write down to the reader, I won't compromise it.

KEVIN: I suppose you come across some poets like Sharon Olds and Billy Collins who can't but do what they do, and you don't ever expect them to break out into a new mode.

PHILIP: I know you're a Billy Collins fan and I can quite enjoy some of his poems. I heard him on the radio, reading. After half an hour I had to turn it off. I couldn't bear it any more, it was all the same kind of poem. And it was appealing to me as a reader, *and* I thought I've had enough of this; the wry appealing humour; all the wit; and it was sort of ingratiating. I couldn't bear it. And Sharon Olds, the most extraordinarily uneven poet. Or is it that 'forceful naiveté' again? Perhaps they are what they are.

KEVIN: The questions about work practices begin with an Auden quote: *when we genuinely speak, we do not have the words ready to do our bidding; we have to find them, and we do not know exactly what we are going to say until we've said it, and we say and hear something new that has never been said or heard before.* Now I suppose that whole statement hinges on the meaning and use and significance of the word: *genuinely.*

PHILIP: It gets back to what I was saying before: I have no interest in repeating myself, let alone anyone else, so I prefer to pursue a 'poetic' and a realisation of it that I feel to be genuine—rather than to write to/for some consistent audience. The work should be as astutely and evocatively mine as it can be. It's not a problem to be solved; it's a finding that is being expressed. The former is 'objective'; the latter is poetry.

KEVIN: How do you find the words to do your bidding?

PHILIP: Well, of course, I don't know the answer to that. That's the easy answer. We can move onto the next question now.

KEVIN: I've got no answer to that, either.

PHILIP: One: things happen to me; and two: things I use are perhaps methods; they're equally natural and they're what I've always found to be productive. Firstly I'll realise I'm hearing words in phrases (mentally) that strike me as true and poetic, they have concentration and insight. Or I'll see or experience something stirring in my 'fascination-nerve'. I think there are only two main ways I'm going to approach this and the first is to begin writing, as the process to find it.

An attraction, then an impulse without a body, then the work that I am in search of. I'm in search of *the poem* that it might lead me to. The poem might embody the initial moment, it might begin but then depart from it, and it might ignore it. Like the Frank O'Hara poem seemingly about oranges, "Why I am not a painter",[10] where it never makes it to the oranges but does make a poem. Such poems are about something but never, actually, about the beginning because the poem becomes more important than the impulse. I hear a phrase or a couple of lines and I write them down. I have been thinking about something, or something's been on my mind, and it starts to coalesce in a phrase or an image.

Secondly, my method is to mine a large theme. Several of my books are, from beginning to end, theme-based books. This initial moment of alertness, visitation, fascination, emotional arresting may prompt me to a larger work. It will at some point form an image. *The Projectionist*[11] was the old, eccentric, even grotesque couple I called the Benchleys. *Sky Poems* was the idea of a desire-world. *The Well Mouth*[12] was *Sky Poems'* opposite: not heaven but limbo, not possibility unlimited but no possibility.

I think about my theme, ponder it, meditate upon it—all those modes for different kinds of mentation; I feel, explore, worry, consider, for a year—maybe for a year and a half—without writing anything. I'm building a massive subconscious pressure of desire and material. Data. I read, I think, I ask myself questions, I keep this theme in mind when I'm looking at other things, and doing other things. I read books and then find the bits in the books that are relevant. I look at films, music, anything.

I deliberately resist writing the poem. It's an act of creative will *not* to write it. I don't want to exhaust it by beginning too early. I resist it to the point where I panic myself, and I panic it into being. I create an encounter which I cannot put off anymore and that encounter, hopefully, has built up such mass, it is such an entity, that it's worth all the build up, except I'm blind to it, it's invisible. If I was run over at this stage there would be nothing. I may have written notes but nothing like a poem.

And then I write it, start writing it and I just write it and write it. I don't re-read, I don't look back. I don't censor and I am fearless. I imagine any manifestation of this theme, anything to know it, embody it, provoke it, and I think nothing other than of its great success. I know it as the continual release and expansiveness of poems arriving. And I maintain that searching. I'm always searching for the potential, the probabilities.

Each of these probabilities might become a complete poem, or a sequence of poems, within the larger theme-of-the-book. The mothership. I might write a whole book, I might write two books, I might write two hundred poems over two or three months. That's what makes the theme books work. If I was run over at this stage, there would be pages and pages of first drafts. And if I lost them, I couldn't re-realise them. I have no memory of their contents. It's scary. It's a scary method.

Thirdly, briefly, with nothing on my mind, I just sit down and start writing. This has sometimes been the unlikely source of the best things I've written. I'm blank, I've no intention whatsoever except to play with the chance beginnings. I sit down and start writing from scratch. First line, who knows? Second line, who knows? Second line makes a third line, the lines feed into each other and I keep writing. In a book of mine I have called this process *feeding the ghost.*

KEVIN: Does music play any role in your writing methods?

PHILIP: Huge. I never listen to music when I'm working, I write in silence. But I think with music going on, I let it carry me as a dynamic, I ask myself questions with music playing and I love music in me. I consider music to be the highest form of existence. Hugely emotional but also unworldly, transcendent.

KEVIN: And do you have a daily regime of writing?

PHILIP: No, not now I have more time. I used to write at night when I was working during the day. Now, I write more during the day and I also have the freedom to write any time in the week, so I write on the weekend, at night, in the day.

KEVIN: But there's no structuring of the day?

PHILIP: No. Except I never write poetry in the morning, I can't do it. And I can't write poetry on a keyboard, I have to write it by hand, I have to feel the ink soaking into the paper of my pad. The pen has to feel smooth but grip without scratching and the ink must be wet enough and the pad paper absorbent enough for this tactile soaking-in to occur. If the ink is dry-ish, or the pen scratches or is too fine, or the paper is too shiny and impermeable, or too rough, forget it.

I like to work alone in the house—if possible—and with no likely noise from the outside world. Prose is interruptible, poetry isn't. Generally

I write in the afternoon and evening. There's one condition to this—unless I'm in that 'heat' moment when I'm writing poem after poem in the big theme books; I can write them any time of the day and night.

KEVIN: So how do you occupy that morning time?

PHILIP: Oh, I fuck about. I waste time; I daydream. I do another form of writing. I do shopping, I muck about, I walk, get out in the street, I read and it wastes time. I play with the cats. Sometimes I prefer to waste time daydreaming, unformed, than let myself see a movie or even let myself read a book. I do a lot of cooking.

KEVIN: Did you miss that time when you were working and teaching?

PHILIP: Oh yeah (joking). But the compensations: you write with varied concentration if you have less time, you write in a different way.

I trust my subconscious; most of my writing comes out of nowhere. I really have no idea where it's coming from. It's why I won't compromise it. And while I hope it articulates an inner speaking, poetry *can* be a selfish little mystery. It has to impress me but also convince me. The question poetry posits is: convince me of what? All the same, I think if it does 'speak', if it is 'convincing' *and* I can keep holding it to those standards, then it's my right work. It's all feeding the ghost. It does mean I'm not trying to please people and that's perhaps my shortcoming. But so it is; I'm serious.

KEVIN: It's hard to tell the difference between a strength and a shortcoming, sometimes.

PHILIP: True, and good writing can be seductive. Once you've acquired the taste.

*   *   *

KEVIN: When you are writing, how quickly do you compose?

PHILIP: Quickly, very quickly. And I rewrite for a long time. I write drafts in one sitting, I'll write a lot. I can write a six-page poem in an afternoon. I could write a whole book in a month.

KEVIN: And how close are they to finished products?

PHILIP: Some will be word for word, almost. When I'm doing this heat work, writing a hundred poems in a month or two, there will be a dozen of them which do not get rewritten. They'll be short poems, admittedly, but they will be almost word for word.

If I start hearing lines and phrases in my head, and I know the poem, where they belong, I know that poem's not finished, or it might be, at least, but I have to take those lines back to it and think okay, do they fit? Now, they might fit and I might have to go back even later and read the whole poem and think no, I was fooling myself, they don't fit. That doesn't happen very often, it's usually in the rewriting, hands on re-reading and rewriting.

So it's a different writer, clearly, who rereads and then rewrites the poem. It's not the same; my first writer is fast and unknown. I'm just simply a cypher, I really am just a conduit, writing stuff down. I don't know until it's coming out on the page and I write as fast as I can write. The poem can come as fast as I can write it down, the difference is *how cleanly* it comes out. If it's messy, it doesn't mean it's any better or worse. Sometimes it just comes out fast and I re-write it fast too. They're all different. But firstly, speed; secondly, slow writing. Then close judgment.

KEVIN: Do you have that feeling of a disconnection from a sense of time when you are involved in that work?

PHILIP: Time's irrelevant, it's gone. I'm also a fidget, and I might be halfway through a fast poem and then I think I've done it for the time being and I just get up and walk around and daydream again. And then I come back and just keep going. So that's different: I will move from one time into another time.

KEVIN: The last question here is, is there anything your readers owe you?

PHILIP: They owe me nothing at all—and I'm sure most people have answered that question in the same way—except for what I was hoping, that openness. I think if they're going to read the work, they owe us all a chance to take it as it is, not as they expect, and not because they read your name and think I will or won't like this. Read it critically but first, just read it openly. They could say *I don't have to like this to read it, I'll just give it a go, and I'll try to read it without prejudice.*

And *I* don't have to keep on with this word 'like'! I can admire someone's work, I might get something from it; I mean there's a lot of art, there's much that happens in the world that I don't exactly like but I can see the value of. Prejudice is a different thing; prejudice is a set way of responding. If poetry *is* the art of inner speaking, we should do it the honour of . . . listening.

PS: Since doing this interview I have selected, edited and re-published poems from *Sky Poems* and *The Well Mouth* alongside a full collection of new poems in *Alterworld*. And I have put aside poetry (temporarily) in favour of fiction.

NOTES

1   Salom, Philip 1980 *The Silent Piano: Poems*, Fremantle: Fremantle Press
2   White, Patrick 1970 *The Vivisector*, Stockholm: Bonniers
3   Thomas, Dylan 1954 *Under Milk Wood*, "First Voice" (read by Richard Burton), London: BBC Radio
4   Salom, Philip 1987 *Sky Poems*, Fremantle: Fremantle Press
5   *The Silent Piano*; *The Projectionist: A Sequence*, Fremantle: Fremantle Press, 1983
6   Lessing, Doris 1994 *Under My Skin*, New York: Harper Collins; and Lessing, Doris 1997 *Walking in the Shade*, New York: Harper Collins
7   Salom, Philip 2010 *The Keepers Trilogy*, Glebe: Puncher and Wattman
8   Salom, Philip 1991 *Playback*, Fremantle: Fremantle Press

9   Salom, Philip 2014 "William Hart-Smith, poet, mentor & friend",
    Australian Poetry Journal 4.1: 29–41
10 O'Hara, Frank 2008 "Why I am not a painter", from *Selected Poems*, edited
    by Mark Ford, New York: Random House
11 Salom, Philip 1980 *The Silent Piano: Poems*, Fremantle: Fremantle Press
12 Salom, Philip 2005 *The Well Mouth*, Fremantle: Fremantle Press

"You can't write if you're cut off from life"
Robyn Rowland

Jan Juc, Victoria

KEVIN: We start from the assumption that any poet is connected to the world. What are your points of connection—for example, a job, or through teaching and education, family, publishers? Which matter to you in your poetic practice?

ROBYN: I thought that was the hardest question on the list. I find it difficult to feel a sense of belonging to the poetry world, as I understand it, in Australia. I came through in the group of women who were young through the 1968 Push:[1] that big thing with the guys, all the big names, and we were kind of inconsequential. And I think I learned that I was inconsequential, in terms of poetry, even though I'd started publishing at 18 in *Overland*.[2] So I went in with Barrie Reid[3] who, for me, was a good connection to poetry. He was encouraging and he liked my work. He made me feel like I was a poet and he worked on a book with me, *Perverse Serenity*.[4] He wrote a wonderful analysis of the book which meant it got published. At the end of it he said, *No-one will like this book in this country*. And I said, *God, why?* He said, *It will be one of the best books published this year. No-one will like it because it's about romantic love and passionate love and Australian poetry just doesn't deal with it.* That was in the early 1980s. It's changed a lot since then, but it made me feel I was riding the boundaries.

I wasn't in a literary university environment but I was involved in literature at the University of New South Wales' Wollongong campus, before it was a university of its own. We had a professor who did not accept that there was an Australian literature. We weren't allowed to study it. So, we created a ruckus about this; eighty per cent of us were involved in the campaign.

KEVIN: Were you doing a BA?

ROBYN: I was doing a BA, and there was a push in English to get Australian lit on the course. He was absolutely opposed to it. He was English and what he did was really clever. At the end of that year he introduced a new grading system which was called a terminating pass. You passed but you weren't allowed to go on to second year English. That was the end of my formal relationship with English literature, which was devastating because I'd loved poetry since I was a kid.

If you were to ask me, how did I first get into poetry, it would be through my father. My father still recites all of the old poets, Banjo Paterson,[5] all of those. We will sit there together, still doing it.

In primary school we had these Readers that included poetry. The first poem—I still remember it—was really luscious, really overdone. It was a poem about nature, and it went, *The Morning Star paled slowly, the Cross hung low to the sea, / And down the shadowy reaches the tide came swirling free.*[6] The song in it really pulled me in.

KEVIN: Another big, general question and a question I'm always curious to know the answer to: what has sustained you in your writing life?

ROBYN: I'm from an old school that believes poetry is not something you *do*, it's something you *be*. For me, I'm not well if I'm not writing, I don't feel well in myself. I don't feel natural or at ease with the world if I'm not. It's a survival thing, there's too much going on in my head and my body, it has to go somewhere; and writing was always it. And it wasn't until I was in my fifties I realised that I started writing as a child, when I was 11, because no one was listening. And I still think I write because I don't think anyone's listening.

I feel that I'm writing to myself, so what sustains me is that. I just love it. I feel alive. It's almost sexual, connecting with language in a really intimate way. It's almost like taking your skin off. There's a feeling that without it you just wouldn't be alive.

When you get rejected for something, that's difficult to deal with because no matter what anybody says, they feel rejected. That's the hard bit, trying to sustain yourself when you've been knocked back. The thing that I don't like most about poetry is there aren't any rules. If there were just some rules, a blueprint, I'd do it. I was a competitive swimmer, so I'd just *try* hard. Poetry is not something you can try hard in. It's either going and it's being accepted, or it's not.

The other thing that sustains me is readings. So when I do readings I know I've hit the mark: I can see it in people's faces. At the moment, I'm doing a lot of that in Turkey. At the end of it people are quite teary and moved. That sustains me. Whether it's good poetry or not is not the question: you know you've done something useful, you've done something worthwhile.

KEVIN: And is that reading in English? Or reading with a translator beside you?

ROBYN: Reading in English. We're doing bilingual readings now, so I read the English and it's up on a screen. Then Mehmet Ali Çelikel reads in Turkish and it's up on the screen in Turkish. So we're doing both languages.

Mehmet is a Turkish academic who's also my translator. It's a whole other exciting world that I can't believe happened. That's the sort of thing that sustains. So first of all, I think there's not a choice and secondly, I think it is responses that sustain me. The only thing that ever stopped me writing was some political work. For nearly twenty years I was involved in campaigns around in vitro fertilisation and genetic engineering. I think you've got two kinds of mind; a structured mind and an unstructured mind. The analytic critical mind had to keep arguing and presenting arguments and reading science. It didn't leave any space for the flowing kind of mind. I experienced that quite strongly.

KEVIN: How does that observation connect with your previous statement that you don't feel well if you don't write?

ROBYN: It's a good question. Well, I wasn't well. I was doing something else. All my life I've had a sense of social commitment. When I was doing the political work it was motivated by a sense of commitment towards social change and the 'right thing', however you would define that. And in poetry there's a similar social commitment for me. Sometimes it comes through in political writing: I'm writing a lot of war poems at the moment. At other times it's about exposure: exposing emotional life, exposing things to make them less fearful to people. And to say, *I've got that too*, or *I've been there too* or, *it's okay*. Here we all are, in the human condition. In a way, there's a continuity and purpose.

KEVIN: Something of what poetry offers you was offered by the political work?

ROBYN: It was, actually. The creative side was in writing journal articles and book chapters. It wasn't like you were without creativity. But you were without silence, you didn't have silence and you didn't have space to let things move, you had to be pushing them and structuring them.

KEVIN: Can you remember where you first encountered poetry?

ROBYN: I remember that school classroom in primary school with that poem. Also Dad used to recite. He can do the lot. He's 94 and he's still doing it. *Clancy of the Overflow*[7] would have to be my favourite, and Dad's favourite. It was so much of a favourite of his that when Ennis, my first son, was a one-year-old, Dad bought him a copy of *Clancy of the Overflow* with pictures. He would read that to him.

KEVIN: So it was very much part of your life. If you were to describe yourself to somebody that you don't know, would you describe yourself or identify yourself as a poet?

ROBYN: It depends what country I'm in. In Ireland I would say I'm a poet. And in Turkey, definitely, I would say I'm a poet. But in Australia, I would say I'm a writer. You end up with these terrible conversations where people say, *Oh I write too* or, *I'm a poet too*. You never get that in Ireland or Turkey. It's not seen as something just anybody can do. In Australia they would say, *What kind of poetry do you write?* And the answer is, *read it and then you'll know*, but you don't say that.

KEVIN: Can you say contemporary poetry? You can't. I try to say that, but I can't.

ROBYN: That doesn't make sense to people, they don't understand. I say, *It's poetry you can understand*. And they say, *About what?* You say, *Life, death, sex, children, war, you know, living*. That's the best you can come up with.

KEVIN: Is that a particularly Australian response?

ROBYN: I find it is. In Ireland people would have read Seamus Heaney's new book. It's part of the cultural heritage. It's turning out to be like that in Turkey as well. The experience in Turkey is different because poets have been jailed, poets have been sent into exile. It has been seen as a powerful form of expression, whereas in Australia you would laugh to think of putting a poet in jail for publishing a poem. People would just laugh. Why would you do that?

KEVIN: Is that because we've been brought up in the background of Banjo Paterson and Henry Lawson and Dorothea Mackellar, the folksy, nationalistic tinge the poetry attracts to itself, rather than a deep political involvement?

ROBYN: As a country, white Australia, the white settlement, hasn't had to really contend with difficult things like civil war or a big war on our land. When I was in Bosnia, the guy who was in charge of the poetry festival there had crawled through the tunnel in Sarajevo many times to get food for his family. That's a different kind of poet. The more you travel the more you realise how easy we have got it.

KEVIN: And you only have to read a bit of Aboriginal poetry to see how difficult it is for some parts of our society. So, poetry provides you with ways to engage with social and political issues?

ROBYN: It does but it's not the prime motivation. That just comes out of life experience. I'm working on a book on Gallipoli poems at the moment and I had no intention of writing them at all. I was doing a poetry reading in Çanakkale, which is opposite Gallipoli, across the Dardanelles. There's an Australian Consulate there and they got me to teach in a Turkish/Australian cultural centre, where I taught some workshops for a few days. When we were talking, I said to the Consul, *I'm not going to go near anything on Gallipoli*. He said, *Thank God*. I said, *Are you well over it?* And he said, *That's all that people associate with Turkey*. So I was doing a whole lot of other poems about Turkey, about Istanbul and places I've been to.

Then I met a young man on the registration desk in the hotel. He asked, *Are you an ANZAC?* That's what people often say, are you ANZAC. I said, *No I'm Australian/Irish*. And he said, *Oh, terrible war*. Then he was telling me about his grandfather. I said, *I'm a poet and sometimes I think I should write about this*. He said, *Oh I have a book for you*. The next day he brought in a book with photographs. It was truly awful. I said, *Tell me about the war*. So I went to the naval museum and I was shocked because the representation of the war was totally different. It actually began with the Çanakkale naval battle—you never hear about it—which the Turks won. Nobody ever told me this. Then I get a personal story and I'm really moved by it. Then I write the poem. It's not like I think to myself, *I must redress the issue of Gallipoli*. It evolved.

KEVIN: How big is that book?

ROBYN: About 84 pages. The poems are bilingual. Both of us [Mehmet Ali Çelikel and I] believe it's important that Turkish and

161

Turkish/Australians and Australians read the stories. A friend of mine in Ireland read the manuscript, and he was blown away because, he said, he thought the poetry was good but he never knew any of this.

It's not like I set out to do it. It will be political because of the position the poems take. They're meant to be written so that if a Turkish person reads them they will be as struck, and as moved, as an Australian reading them because they speak the same language. It's a tall order, but I got into it without even thinking it's a tall order.

I wrote a poem called *Red Threads* about the Stolen Generations;[8] the kids who were taken. I didn't set out to do that, but it had made me angry for three or four years and I couldn't write it because I was too angry. I read in the paper about a man telling a story of when he was taken. He was the same age as one of my boys. He said this line, *I hid in the long grass*. I could just see my sons at the same age, about 7, hiding in the long grass. That's how I went in.

That's the poetic process, that's the thing you can't teach. You can teach loads of other stuff, but there are some things you can't teach. You can alert people to observational skills, but you can't teach them.

KEVIN: Continuing on the theme of travel, are there ways in which you find your writing is changed by being at home or away from home or moving?

ROBYN: It does. Landscape is important in my work. I hadn't realised that for ages, I just did it. It's like my whole body actually enters the landscape: I don't observe it, I'm actually in it.

KEVIN: Which is what Ted Hughes did with animals, I guess.

ROBYN: Entering them. With Irish culture and landscape, you would think there would be something happening because I'm third generation Irish, but it's still peculiar that it does happen. You wouldn't expect it with Turkey and yet it seems to happen there too. The work changes, I pick up the rhythms of that poetry. Since I've been living in Ireland part-time, it's different, I would describe it as lyric narrative poetry. Some of them are quite long, like epics. That's standard in Irish traditional work and it's not as though I set out to do it. And in Turkey, I've picked up some rhythm, some way of speaking.

KEVIN: Are you learning Turkish?

ROBYN: I have some Turkish, but I'm not going to learn it too perfectly because the imperfection of your Turkish is what connects you to the Turks. Mehmet pointed out that I include Turkish words in the poems. That must be an absorption process that I don't understand.

KEVIN: What about the wider cultural history, the treatment of women?

ROBYN: In the early days I used to write strongly feminist poems. When I came to do the *New and Selected*,[9] and I looked at it, I'd left them all out. All of them. They were too vicious, to me, to read. I don't know how people read them, they're strong, but they're so on the bone. There's a couple about rape where I've taken actual rapes that were so horrible. I couldn't put them in. Since the burn-out and the breast cancer I can't handle things too vicious or mean. I hope I haven't lost that feminist edge, but I'm not looking for that story anymore; I think it comes through anyway.

*　　*　　*

KEVIN: How relevant is your education to the type of poetry that you've ended up writing? After you couldn't do literature anymore, what did you move on to study?

ROBYN: I was doing psychology, history and philosophy of science. I always loved history, ancient history. That comes through in the poetry. I started a magazine in the University of Wollongong with two other people, Trevor Irwin and John Broomhall. It was called *Poems in Public Places*. So clever, weren't we, because we had the L put up, so it looked like *Poems in Pubic Places*. Oh, it was so witty. We published a lot of fine poets who were writing then. That meant I kept writing, and I actually was almost freed by not having to do literature.

I started teaching Women's Studies—we were creating Women's Studies then. You could read *all* of Women's Studies literature, it was so small. Adrienne Rich, Marge Piercy, Gwen Harwood . . .

KEVIN: Diane Wakoski.[10]

ROBYN: Yeah, and Judith Wright. We were in the process of re-finding the women poets. But those Americans had a big impact on me. My all-time favourite American poet must be—because whenever I teach workshops I always go back to him—Robert Frost. Frost has this narrative lyric thing too and it's quite moving. That poem, *Birches*,[11] about the boy climbing out on the birches full of ice and snow. There's this beautiful description and then he's off. Before all the talk about snow and storms came in, this boy who lives too far from town to play cricket is climbing out in the birch. He talks about the branch coming down to the ground from the boy's weight on it. Then he says, I would love to be doing that, but let no God mistake and leave me in heaven, *earth's the best place for love, no doubt about it.* At the end it says, *one could do worse than be a swinger of birches.* The whole poem moves through a number of different stories.

KEVIN: Turning to the matter of other poets: have you had poet friends? Is it important that you feel part of a community even if you are an outsider?

ROBYN: I will always feel an outsider, I think.

KEVIN: You do have some longstanding friends in the poetry world though.

ROBYN: I do; currently, and in the past. I had a close friendship with Jenny Harrison; for many years we would read each other's work. Every six weeks we met, drank far too much champagne and read each other's work. That was good. I really miss that. In Ireland I had a poetry circle with some people, that become a triangle that became a line, then disappeared. I feel the absence of that. I would like that.

Now I work with Alex Skovron, who will often read poems for me. He is just absolutely wonderful. He has that capacity to crawl inside what you're trying to do. I've a friend in Ireland, Paul Casey, I do that with sometimes. It's really useful feedback as well. Every now and then there'll be the odd other person, you know; it might be Gina Mercer in Tasmania who has got a great ear and a great eye. I've another friend, Ita in Ireland. But I do miss that. I'd love to have it regularly again. But it's hard to find people you trust.

KEVIN: And how do you respond to their comments when their comments are not wholly positive?

ROBYN: I love it. Actually, it's not that they're not wholly positive—I wouldn't send them a poem I thought was really bad—but I don't see their responses as not being positive. I like being edited. I like having people give me feedback. So many times they put their finger on the one thing that you're uncertain about. I'm honoured that people would bother because it's time-consuming.

*   *   *

KEVIN: So are there any particular effects you would like to have on your readers?

ROBYN: I want them to feel. And I want them to shift. I want them to understand something in the poem, and shift or be opened somehow. Say it was the breast cancer poems, it would be towards understanding what that was about; or the poems on depression. What I find weird about that is that the poems on depression and breast cancer, you'd think the people who had breast cancer and depression wouldn't want to read those, but actually they're the ones they want.[12]

KEVIN: And often it's a surprise.

ROBYN: Mostly it's a surprise. It's a real surprise. The things people like.

KEVIN: We've got that Auden quote at the beginning, *When we genuinely speak, we don't have the words ready to do our bidding, we have to find them and we do not know exactly what we're going to say until we've said it and we say and hear something new that has never been said or heard before.* What's your response to that? And how do you find the words to do your bidding?

ROBYN: There is a process that I've uncovered over the years. First of all, it's living the life, with all its blemishes and its highs and lows. You can't write if you're cut off from life. You've got to be observing as you go along. Then you write the odd notes down. It's taking the notes, and it can be loads of time later before you ever use it. It's not a decision to write the poem, I think. Sometimes you sit down, and something's urged you to do it. Then you start the poem. Then the words find you. It's like meditation, or like prayer. It's an altered state. I described it once as self-goneness. The self is gone, and you only know the self is gone when you've come back to the self.

I love the bit where you've got the skeleton of the poem and sometimes it's got flesh on it and sometimes it hasn't. Then there's the lovely rewriting stage. Then the editing, which nobody loves. You have to carve things out, and for me there's usually three extra lines at the end because I lectured all those years and I just want to make sure everyone got the point.

KEVIN: Do you find material in conversations and take what other people say? And how do you feel about doing that?

ROBYN: I think you collect wherever it is. Newspapers are great. They often give first person accounts, so you'll often hear dialogue. Like that guy saying, *I hid in the long grass.* They're great triggers. You have to be careful with it. You're absorbing stuff all the time so you need to make sure that you're honest about what you're doing; and anyone can make a slip. I do try to acknowledge where I've picked up something.

KEVIN: How do you acknowledge it? In a footnote?

ROBYN: A footnote, yeah.

KEVIN: Do you think it spoils the effect of the poem to have a footnote?

ROBYN: I don't like footnotes generally. But you've got to have a note somewhere to say it's a line from someone else, don't you?

KEVIN: Sometimes you can have those notes at the back, can't you?

ROBYN: With the Gallipoli book,[13] there's so much material, the best idea is that whoever publishes it, you put the references on their website.

KEVIN: That's a good idea. Do you have critical voices that you rely on or that you conjure, particularly when you're doing your editing work?

ROBYN: Do you mean critics who've written about poetry?

KEVIN: It could be critics or it could be, for example, adopting an Alex Skovron view of your poem or a Jennifer Harrison view of your poem.

ROBYN: No, I don't. I try to hear it from Robyn Rowland's point of view and whether it's working for me.

* * *

KEVIN: Thinking of the act of writing, would you say you have to be in the right mood to compose? Or in no mood.

ROBYN: I've been talking about the process, so it's not like a mood. It's this experience of self-goneness, I have to be like that.

KEVIN: So when you go to the desk, you're not in that state are you?

ROBYN: Sometimes I am. Sometimes, but no. With the history poems it's even more complicated. I have to embed myself in the history, so I might spend two days watching videos, terrible stuff, the photographs and I might do eye witness accounts of the Bosnian War . . .

KEVIN: Do you watch that material on YouTube?

ROBYN: You can get quite a bit on YouTube. You can get films that you never think you'd see. There's one on Gallipoli that was put out by a Turkish filmmaker that's brilliant, actually. I do a lot of research for the war poems, trying to find the voices. Then I want the facts to be correct. So I do loads of that. Then when I'm swimming in it almost, when it's hard things like war, I'm almost vomiting because life in the trenches was so horrendous in its detail. Then you think, I've had enough, I've got to get the poem out. I've got to because I'll just go mad. And then start. Where do you start? You don't think where you start, you just enter. You're already in it and then it just comes. Doesn't it?

KEVIN: Yes it does. It does.

ROBYN: Just comes, weirdly like that.

KEVIN: Are composing and coming up with the right edits similar processes to you?

ROBYN: Not really. Not really. The composition has four points—the observation, the writing down, the self-goneness, the editing. Editing has more distance in it. You're stepping back and taking a really good look and reading it out loud and hearing it go clunk where it goes clunk. But I like that process. It's a different experience. You're bringing a different kind of mind to it, really. I like tidying up, although I look chaotic.

KEVIN: No, it doesn't look chaotic. So does music play a role?

ROBYN: I don't think I would ever write with music going. I know a lot of musicians. I probably know almost more musicians than poets, so, yeah it does, it does have a big role.

KEVIN: And have you played an instrument?

ROBYN: I played Irish music for some time, I played Bodhran—it's a drum. I used to play for set dances, and I was very good. I played fiddle for a while, but I've got a lot of neck problems. I played piano when I was a kid, so I like a whole range of music. I had a band called Funky Mammas when the kids were little. I wish I could play more and I wish I could sing.

KEVIN: Your poetry is a kind of singing.

ROBYN: Oh, thank you, Kevin.

KEVIN: So just a quick question to finish with: when you're writing, why do you stop writing?

ROBYN: Ah, because I'm hungry! When I stop writing, I stop because I've other obligations in life.

KEVIN: But then how do you know when you've finished a poem?

ROBYN: That's a good question. You feel it. You just feel it's finished, that's done. Sometimes I wish, with the longer poems I keep thinking, *stop now, stop now, stop now,* but it's not finished yet. So, for me, there almost has to be an automatic sense of a middle, a beginning, an end.

NOTES

1 The Push was a left-wing intellectual and literary group in Sydney active from the late 1940s to the early 1970s

2 *Overland*, established in 1954, is an Australian literary and cultural magazine

3 Reid was also the youngest contributor to *Angry Penguins*, the modernist literary journal of the 1940s. During his life he contributed to many literary journals including *Meanjin*, was editor of literary journals including *Overland*, wrote about Australian art, and published a collection of his poems entitled *Making Country*. Reid was friends with the artists at Heidi (John and Sunday Reid, the Blackmans) and lived at Heidi when Robyn knew him.

4 Rowland, Robyn 1990 *Perverse Serenity*, Port Melbourne, Victoria: Heinemann

5 Andrew Barton 'Banjo' Paterson is an Australian bush poet. Paterson's first poem was published in *The Bulletin* in 1885. Paterson's first collection, *The*

Man from Snowy River, and Other Verses (1895), was received with great
acclaim. Paterson wrote Australia's best-known folk song, 'Waltzing Matilda

6 Cuthbertson, James Lister 1907 'The Australian Sunrise', from *An Anthology of Australian Verse*, Sydney: Angus and Robertson
7 Paterson, AB 1982 [1889] *Clancy of the Overflow, or The Bushman in the City*, Adelaide: Paul Rigby
8 The Stolen Generations are the children of Australian Aboriginal and Torres Strait Islander people who, under Acts of Parliament, were forcibly taken from their families and communities between 1910 and 1970
9 Rowland, Robyn 2010 *Seasons of Doubt and Burning: New and Selected Poems*, Parkville: Five Islands Press
10 Adrienne Rich (1929–2012), US poet and essayist; Marge Piercy, US poet and novelist; Gwen Harwood (1920–1995), Australian poet and librettist; Diane Wakoski, US poet, essayist and teacher at Michigan State University; Judith Wright (1915–2000), Australian poet and environmentalist
11 Frost, Robert 1916 'Birches', in *The Poetry of Robert Frost*, edited by Edward Connery Lathem, New York: Holt Rinehart and Winston
12 'The Great Way is not difficult . . .', the last section of *Fiery Waters* (Wollongong: Five Islands Press, 2001), is a sequence of poems on breast cancer; poems in *Silence and its Tongues* (Wollongong: Five Islands Press, 2006) address cancer and depression
13 *This Intimate War: Gallipoli/Çanakkale 1915 – İçli Dışlı Bir Savaş: Gelibolu/ Çanakkale 1915* (with Turkish translations by Mehmet Ali Çelikel), Parkville: Five Islands Press, 2014

"A lot of accident about it"
Ron Pretty

Melbourne, Victoria

KEVIN: Ron, I'm going to start with a question that's not on the sheet here. Just to throw you off. Make it as spontaneous as possible. What has sustained you through your life and work as a poet?

RON: I think, in part the actual pleasure of writing itself. One of the great pleasures of my life is still to sit out on the balcony or to sit in a quiet room somewhere with a glass of wine and a fountain pen and a pad. I can sit there for three or four hours quite happily. Sometimes I write poetry and sometimes I just sit there. But that's always been a great pleasure to me; I would rather do that than just about anything. Other things: the friendship of other poets has been important; the support of my family has been important; publication's been important. The fact that people have been prepared to publish what I've written is, I think, important as a kind of verification that what you're doing has some value. I think they're the main things.

KEVIN: So, that's almost as if you *would* write, regardless of an audience.

RON: Yes. Yes, I would. Look, in fact, about three quarters of the time that's exactly what I do. I've got a reject pile at home which is well over 500 poems long. They're poems that I've written at night and when I come down the next morning to have a look at them, I realise they just aren't going to fly. If I type them up at all—and I don't always type them up if they're that bad, and they sometimes are—if I type them up and still think that they're no good, I put them in the reject pile.

So, yes, they don't have any kind of audience, excepting me, briefly. But for the other poems, audience becomes important. You try to think, *who might be interested in this poem*? And you think, *I could send this poem to Deb Westbury[1] because she likes to see what I'm writing*. And that's been important to me. Is this a poem that might be published? Well, if so, where might it go? Those kinds of questions.

KEVIN: And just for curiosity's sake, how many drafts before you give up on a poem?

RON: Sometimes first draft. I can tell, the moment I look at it the next morning, that it's no good. Years ago, when I was teaching at Casino High School, Les Murray came through as a visiting poet, I remember asking him, *how do you avoid polishing a poem to death*? And it's still a question for me. I still sometimes find that I work on a poem and I work on a poem and I work, and it just doesn't go anywhere. So, giving up is sometimes a long way in, sometimes very quick.

KEVIN: Can you pinpoint the things that have gone wrong or are inadequate about those poems you abandon?

RON: Yes, sometimes. Sometimes they're self-indulgent. Sometimes they're poems I'm writing that I've written many times before, and in better versions. Sometimes they're poems that have too many clichés and stock-phrases in them. Usually it is one of those three things.

KEVIN: And the poems that you continue to work on, that you send out for publication, what's gone right with them? In contrast?

RON: That's a harder question. There's something that you've enjoyed writing in them, and that you enjoy re-reading in them. There's an exploration in there, or an imagery, a pattern of imagery that's interesting. Sometimes it's as simple as saying it's in a form you think other people will respond to, that other people will get enjoyment from.

But you've got to get enjoyment from it yourself, you've got to think that there's something interesting going on in it for you as a writer, before you even ask whether it's important for anybody else. One of the great pleasures of writing is that sometimes you write things which you haven't expected to write. And you get a real surprise about what, in fact, you have written. There's a comment in *For Whom the Bell Tolls*,[2] a comment by Hemingway, in which he says, *I always try to write as well as I can; sometimes I get lucky and write better than I can.* That's spot on. That's what happens and when you've done that, when you've found that there's something really interesting in the poem going on, they're the ones that you're likely to keep.

KEVIN: Almost by definition, that requires a whole lot of duds.

Let's get back to the scheduled questions. We start from the assumption that any poet is connected to the world. What are your points of connection to the world?

RON: Family is obviously important; friends are obviously important. Politics are important. What's going on in the world, your observations of what's going on in the world.

KEVIN: Are they important to you in your poetic practice?

RON: Yes, they are. Your observations of people in the world, I think are very important. I've got a series of poems about politics, which sometimes are successful and sometimes aren't. But I'm still trying to find a way to do that effectively. That's hard, but necessary. Necessary for me, anyway. Politics is an important point of connection to the world.

KEVIN: Can you remember where you first encountered poetry?

RON: I can actually. I was in third class at Sutherland Primary School and I was caned because I couldn't remember the second stanza of 'I was a Pirate Once'.[3]

KEVIN: And how does that stanza go, Ron?

RON: I can remember the first stanza, but I still can't remember the second. It starts with, *I was a hunter once*. I can remember that bit, but I can't remember the rest of it.

KEVIN: So corporal punishment didn't work?

RON: It didn't work in either way. It didn't help me remember the poem. Mind you, remembering poems is very important, and being able to recite poems is very important, but it didn't help me do that, nor did it turn me off poetry.

Although I didn't write any poetry until I got to university, I wrote some short stories. There are some stories in the Sydney Technical High School magazine that I wrote, but I didn't really start writing poetry until I got to university and discovered WB Yeats. For a lot of years—some people would say still—I wrote bad imitations of WB Yeats. He was the person who really started me writing poetry.

KEVIN: Were you consciously imitating him? Was that your aim?

RON: I don't think I was consciously imitating; I think it's that thing about if you haven't read much poetry you tend to imitate those people that you have read.

KEVIN: So how much poetry do you read now; and how regularly do you read poetry?

RON: I read quite a lot. I don't often read a book from cover to cover unless I'm reviewing it for a magazine. I do a little bit of reviewing for *Sotto, Australian Poetry Limited*.[4] I read whole collections when I'm writing a blurb for them. Through the South Coast Writers Centre,[5] I sometimes write paid reviews of books of poetry. Beyond that I tend to dip into poetry and poets that I've come across or poets I've decided I want to read more of. At present I'm reading Pablo Neruda. I've never intensively read Pablo Neruda, so I'm having a look at what he's doing; I dip into him two or three times a week. People whose poetry I like, when a new book comes out, I tend to have a look at. So, I would be reading some poetry three or four days a week.

KEVIN: And what are you making of Pablo Neruda?

RON: Interesting in a number of different ways. He's got a huge range, that's the first thing you notice about him, that he can talk about very domestic things and he'll talk about huge political things. He can be quite romantic, he can be quite political. I'm only reading him in translation, so I'm not sure that I'm getting the full lyrical and sound quality of the poetry, but I'm enjoying it and liking mainly the range, and the way he can deal with that range of topics in his poetry.

KEVIN: We might come back to that question of range. If you were to describe yourself to a stranger, would you be likely to identify yourself as a poet?

RON: I saw that question and wondered what I would answer to it. Not unless they asked me what I did. If it was somebody who was actually interested in what I was doing I'd say I was a writer and leave it at that unless they then said *what kind of writer are you*, in which case I'd say I was a poet.

But then that next question, *what kind of poet are you*, is a question I find difficult to answer. I'm not a particularly lyric poet. I write some narrative poetry. I write a lot of poetry of observation of people. I don't know what sort of poetry you'd call that.

KEVIN: You write from dreams and memory?

RON: Occasionally. I've written some poems from dreams, but they'd be a fairly small minority. I write quite a lot from memory; I'm still writing poems that go back to the time I was in Greece. I don't often go much further back than that.

KEVIN: Are there ways in which you find your writing is changed by being at home or by being away from home?

RON: Being away is quite productive. I write at home, but I find that if I'm home for any long periods of time I gradually decrease the amount I'm writing. And then when I go away again, there's a sudden burst of energy and a burst of writing. Just being in a new environment seems to become very productive for me, even though I don't write about that environment much. I spent six months in Rome, and there aren't many Roman poems in that collection, but there was a lot of new poetry.

KEVIN: Do you think that's to do with the fact that you're writing poetry, or do you think that's more a general effect that new places have on writers and writing?

RON: I think the latter. A change of scenery is always useful as a way of getting a new perspective on things and looking at things at home in a different perspective. I don't think that comes from travel per se. I find that if I go on a trip, I wouldn't expect I'd write much poetry. It's a different kind of experience, being in one new place for some time.

KEVIN: I've experienced that kind of thing too. Let's move on to the question of education. How relevant, do you think, is a person's education to the type of poetry they end up writing? And how relevant was your education to your poetic practice?

RON: My education? Not very. Apart from the fact that it introduced me to Yeats, and a few other poets, in the first couple of years of English I did at Sydney. Not very.

My experience of being in the world has had a far greater impact on me than any formal education I've had. For some writers, particularly these days when so many people are going through university courses, the level of education they get in university has become important as part of the writer's way of approaching the subject.

Sometimes it can be negative. I've seen people who've done doctorates and have stopped writing as a result of doing the doctorate. Other people—I think of somebody like Chloe Wilson⁶—it's been remarkably effective for her; she's writing terrific poetry now, having done that doctorate. I don't know what makes that difference. Perhaps it's the ability to do your own thing, despite what you're learning. To be able to incorporate what you're learning into your own best practice, rather than be controlled by what you're learning.

KEVIN: Often that's a delicate thing to manage. Even when students are highly enthusiastic, there's the management of the question of whether they're going to lose their identity in their enthusiasm or whether they're going to use that enthusiasm to bring originality to what they're doing.

RON: 'To what they're doing', that's right. And to what extent they're influenced in their practice by the practice of the person that's teaching them too. That's sometimes a factor.

KEVIN: A dangerous thing for teachers. You've said a little bit about other poets. Do you want to expand on the importance of other poets to your poetic practice? Your poet friends, when, and are they, important?

RON: At the beginning I had a small group. Deb Westbury, her then-husband, Rob Hood, James Wieland. He was one of the best poets who never published a book. I only saw a few poems that he wrote, but he was really good. There were a group of us who used to meet on a regular basis for a couple of years.

Beyond that, I don't think there's anybody I actually work with on my poetry now. I send poetry to Deb, but not really for comment. I worked for a while with the Youngstreet poets in Sydney,[7] but I found that they didn't really make many comments that were useful to me, mainly I think because there were so many people there, we didn't spend enough time with each poem. But, some poets have been important. When I was in Greece I came across George Seferis,[8] and I was absolutely blown away by him. I think he's an interesting poet.

KEVIN: Was there a teacher in your life who was important to your development? In terms of your life as a poet?

RON: The person who was most important to me was a history teacher at Teachers College, Mr Copley. He made history come alive and, as you probably noticed there's quite a lot of history in my poetry. He made me excited about history and that fed into my poetry.

I can remember a fifth class primary school teacher, a Mr Neil, whom I liked very much. He gave me a lot of confidence as a person. That year I'd had appendicitis which turned into peritonitis. I was in hospital and away from school for about three months. When I came back he really made me feel welcome, and really helped me adjust back into school. I remember him with a great deal of gratitude.

KEVIN: And does history form part of your general reading now?

RON: Very much so. And I read pretty widely. I just finished writing a not very good poem about Robespierre. I read pretty widely around the French Revolution and around the Russian Revolution and all the period in between those two things. European history mainly, from the ancient Greeks and Romans, through to the mid-nineteenth century; well, until the Russian Revolution really, and the Second World War.

KEVIN: Does travelling in Europe bring that alive for you in new ways?

RON: Travelling around Europe, places like Greece and Sicily, brings back ancient history vividly. Not so much modern history, I haven't really travelled to the war sites or any of that.

KEVIN: In what ways is your professional involvement as a writer with publishers, agents, university courses, bookstores, writers' centres, writing groups, useful to you?

RON: A publisher is obviously very useful, and magazine publishers particularly. They keep you going really, particularly magazine publishers, they do the month-by-month keeping you in the scene, as it were, by occasionally accepting a poem. The people who publish books, they're important to you because having a book out is a pretty exciting process. I work a fair bit with the South Coast Writers Centre, and that keeps me in touch with South Coast writers, but I'm more there in a role of a mentor, though I do get quite a lot out of it myself.

KEVIN: And coming back to your practice, do you still have people who comment on early drafts?

RON: No I don't, and I miss that. Having somebody who really knows what you're trying to do and respects what you're trying to do, but is critical of it, is valuable; and I don't have it at present.

KEVIN: And that's more of an accident than a deliberate thing?

RON: Yes, it is. In Wollongong where I am, there isn't anybody I can use in that kind of way.

KEVIN: And Sydney is too far away.

RON: It really is too far away. I spend more time travelling backwards and forwards than I actually spend there. It's too big a group to do much intensive work. You have a quick look at one poem and you've travelled four hours to do it. It's not a great deal of use. I wanted to organise something with Brook Emery,[9] who I'd have really liked to have worked with, but he's in Sydney and the travel made it all imprac-tical. This is one of the things I miss about Melbourne.

KEVIN: Were there poets you were able to work with in Melbourne?

RON: I did. With you, at times . . .

KEVIN: I remember us discussing some poems.

RON: A little bit with Connie Barber,[10] a little bit with Alex Skovron.[11] Alex was a terrific value to me in editing the last book I did. We sat down for a day and worked through a manuscript. If I were still living in Melbourne I think I would use that much more than I can at present.

KEVIN: Some poets with that question have said that comments on early drafts were something they needed as younger writers, as devel-oping writers, and they began then to do that for themselves.

RON: For themselves; I think that's probably true. As I said to you ear-lier, when we started out, I had that group around me in Wollongong with Deb and Rob Hood[12] and John Scott.[13] Maybe I don't need it as much now, although sometimes it'd be nice to say whether a poem is working or not.

KEVIN: Are there any particular effects you want to be having on your readers?

RON: That's a good question. I want, first of all, the reader to be prepared to follow the exploration that's involved in the poem. They've got to be interested enough in what you're doing, I would hope, to actually follow the line of logic through the poem. That's the main thing and you would hope that, if you were surprised by something about the poem, they would be too. You would hope that the emotional content of the poem would be something that they could feel, that they could relate to. You would hope that if the poem was about a particular kind of person or a particular person, fictional or real, that they would respond to that person in a way that the poem has structured. But really, you want them to enjoy the thing, you want them to want to read the next poem, having read that one.

KEVIN: So let's have a look at that Auden quote.

RON: That's an interesting quote. It almost verges on self-contradiction in that he says, and I agree, I never know where the poem's going to go and how it's going to turn out and so on. But he says, *we do not know exactly what we're going to say until we've said it. But we say and hear something new that has never been said or heard before.* Now, how do we know that it's going to be new if we don't know what we're going to say? There is that edge of self-contradiction about it, but I take the point he's making, and I agree with that.

Poetry ought to be an exploration for you as well as for the reader and often I don't know where it's going to go when I start off writing it. I don't know where it's going to turn out. That's one of the things that keeps me writing poetry. There's an element of surprise about the whole process, for me as a writer, and you hope that surprise feeds through to the reader as well.

KEVIN: Yet not knowing where it's going to go, it still goes; how do you find the words that make it go?

RON: A lot of the time it doesn't go. I don't find the words, and then I think I've found the words, but when I look at it again, they haven't taken me anywhere. I find them by accident. I find them by following the logic of the poem as it unfolds. I think often a rhythm or an image or an echo will give me the next line of the poem. And you don't know how that's going to relate to the meaning of the poem, but that's part of the problem, because sometimes it doesn't relate to the meaning of the poem, and the poem explodes or implodes. But when it works, the logic of the sound, of the patterning, develops with the meaning of the poem, and you get something that you hadn't expected before. There is a lot of accident about it.

KEVIN: That's a beautiful description. Do you find material in conversations and overheard speech?

RON: Yes I do. It can be tricky. Sometimes it gives you a totally different character but sometimes you get something that you've thought of before.

KEVIN: It gives you a persona.

RON: Yes. It gives you a persona. Sometimes the conversational elements take over the poem and it deaden it. You've got to be careful of that. Sometimes you're better off paraphrasing the conversation, rather than trying to take it in word for word.

KEVIN: How do you feel about taking things that you've heard?

RON: I don't have a problem with it. If it's something that I've read, I will try to acknowledge it, as long as I remember where I got it from. But if it's something I've heard in casual conversation, I don't have a problem with that. Unless the person could identify themselves from the poem.

I've written a couple of poems recently that I can't do anything with because they're based on a story that somebody told me. I can't now publish that story because they would recognise it. I've enjoyed writing the poem and I think it's a good poem, but it's not a poem I can send anywhere.

KEVIN: So there's a personal or an ethical issue?

RON: There's an ethical issue. If you have a relationship with that person, you don't want to spoil it. There is also that question that you've taken somebody else's story and you've developed it. It's *their* story. You don't really have a right to it. Even though you've enjoyed making something of it that perhaps they would never make of it, and there's that element to it as well, but it's their story.

KEVIN: Because it's their personal story.

RON: It's the story they've told you, so they in fact have a moral right to that story. I don't think you can simply take their story and make it your own poem, can you?

KEVIN: I don't think everyone assumes an ownership of every story they tell you.

RON: That's the kind of thing that I'm talking about. There's a personal element there, a personal issue.

KEVIN: In some ways it can be an archetypal story? And in some ways it's a highly personal story?

RON: And I've written it as an archetypal story, but it's so clearly identifiable that I don't think I can use it.

KEVIN: One of the things I find curious about your poetry, is that every now and again, there are highly personal elements. I'm not sure if you're talking about a situation, or if you're being confessional.

RON: A lot of those things are fictional; things I have created out of a sense of that situation, and personalised to make it about individuals. There's not many of them like that story I was just telling you about, that are actually based on a real event.

KEVIN: Do you give the reader clues when it is fiction? Because we know that a lot of people read poetry highly literally. They see the poet and the voice of the poem as the same thing. I'm guilty of that too.

RON: It's hard to avoid sometimes. Sometimes it's very difficult to tell whether you're dealing with a fiction or a memoir. I don't think I give very many clues about that. I just hope people will assume that what they're reading is fiction.

*   *   *

KEVIN: Are any languages other than English important to your poetic practice?

RON: In translation, but not directly. Greek was important for a long time, but I've lost most of my Greek now. Other than that, not really, and even that's pretty marginal. Music's very important. I write often to classical music and, consciously or unconsciously, I think I'm trying to recapture some of the rhythms and tonal patternings of music. Not the formal structures, I've never tried to write a fugue, a poem as a fugue or anything like that. But I think the rhythmic patterns, the tonal patterns of music, I'm trying to get into the sound quality of the poetry that I'm writing.

KEVIN: Can you tell when you've achieved that?

RON: In some ways you can't tell whether you've achieved anything. What you're trying to do in any poem, after having done a number of drafts, is to decide if the poem is actually working in the way you wanted it to work.

KEVIN: Are there any critical voices you rely on?

RON: No, I don't think so. There are critics that I admire. Martin Duwell is a terrific critic.[14] I like reading his stuff. I like Geoff Page for his generosity.[15] He's a much kinder critic than a lot, but he's also quite perceptive, I think he's a good critic. I don't think I rely on them in any sense, but I admire what they do. There's Coetzee.[16] Some of his stuff is quite interesting.

KEVIN: Yeah, he's a subtle thinker. So, would you say you have to be in the right mood to write poetry?

RON: I think you create your mood. It's a process of sitting down with a clear head, with not much noise going on around me, sometimes with music, with a glass of red and a pen and paper and you start to write and you get into the mood through the act of writing.

KEVIN: And it's writing by hand?

RON: Very much: writing by fountain pen.

KEVIN: Into books that you keep?

RON: I keep them, but I tend not to look at them. I've never thought I wanted to send them to an archive or anything like that. There's too much stuff that I wouldn't want anybody to read. At present I'm working out of a pad, out of a spiral bound folder. I'll often use just ordinary notepad and throw the stuff away when I've finished with it. I don't try and keep it.

KEVIN: You don't harvest it for lines and images for other poems?

RON: No, that's what I use my reject pile for. Every now and then I go through that to see if there's a phrase or a line or a stanza or something that I can take and use somewhere else, but not the handwritten stuff.

KEVIN: In so far as you see composition as a matter of working with emotions—if you do—does composition feel like it involves intense working through of your own emotions or is it more about working out how to elicit them from others?

RON: Emotion is only one of the things you're working with. The question suggests that, but you've got to keep it in perspective too. There's all sorts of things you're working with. You're working with imagination, you're working with intellect, you're working with imagery, you're working with history, you're working with observation, you're working with memory, and rhythm, and sound patterning.

Emotion is one of the things mishandled by a lot of new poets. They tend to tell you what emotion the poem is meant to produce for you instead of finding a way to elicit it. There's got to be something in the poem which will elicit emotion from the language, the incidents, the events of the poem, the imagery of the poem, and not simply be asserted in the poem. But that's as true for me as a writer as it is for the reader as well. It's got to work for me on that level as well.

KEVIN: How quickly do you write?

RON: First draft, very quickly. When I'm really writing fluently, I will write three or four or five drafts in a night, of different poems, of new poems. So each poem is taking me twenty minutes maybe to get down as a first draft on paper.

KEVIN: How quickly do you move from first draft to finished poem?

RON: That varies. Sometimes you immediately throw it out so it doesn't take you any time at all. I write the poem at night and then next day I'll sit down and type it up, or I'll start to type it up, and if I think it's not going anywhere I'll simply discard it at that point. But if I type it up, I'll then have a look and see how close I think it is to being finished. A poem that I finished recently—at least I think it's finished now—has been through five or six major rewrites beyond all of the other fiddling with the edges that I've done. It must have gone through twenty drafts.

KEVIN: And are those drafts on computer?

RON: Yeah.

KEVIN: And do you save versions?

RON: I've got five versions of that saved.

KEVIN: The composing of the initial draft, and then the process of editing, rewriting, redrafting: are they similar processes for you, or different?

RON: They're different processes. The first draft is, in some strange way, fairly unconscious. You're just following whatever comes. I've written enough poems now to be able to guide that process without being particularly conscious of what I'm doing in the guiding. I'm not really thinking too closely about what I'm doing, whether I'm breaking the lines or whether I'm repeating myself or whether some of the images are contradictory. I'm not really thinking along those questions at all, I'm just letting the poem go where it wants to go.

Once you've typed it up you start looking to see if lines contradict each other. The rhythm in that line is too different from the rhythm in that line, you can't have them both like that. And so you are consciously thinking about rhythm, you're consciously thinking about patterning, you're consciously thinking about what's the best kind of line break for this poem, where should I break these lines, so they're much more conscious decisions and you are using your knowledge of metrics, your knowledge of line breaks and the possibilities of line breaks fairly consciously at that point.

KEVIN: And is the look of the poem on the page important to you?

RON: Yes, it is. You can see the way you want it to look on the page, and it's important that it looks that way. This latest poem that I was talking about that I've done all these drafts for, has now finished up in a form that I've not used before. It's in couplets, long line couplets, with a large caesura in the middle of it; it's almost like Anglo Saxon verse in its appearance on the page. It's about myth, in part. It seemed to be the way it needed to be in its final draft, if it is in its final draft. Often the question of making stanzas is at least in part about the appearance of the poem on the page. I don't write many poems that are scattered all over the page, but I still think the appearance on the page is very important.

KEVIN: When you read contemporary poets, do you sometimes recognise an underwritten poem? A poem that needed more work?

RON: You see it a lot. I think the rush to publication, and I'm as guilty as anybody else; the rush to publication is a problem. We tend to send stuff out before we're really sure that it's finished.

When you get to the stage where anything you write can get published, you are in trouble. And I think you see that in poets. You see it in older poets who have really made their name and they are publishing stuff that really, if they were sending it in as unknown poets, would never get published.

KEVIN: There's no general principles or experiences you can point to for when a poem is finished?

RON: No, I don't think there is. I think it's a gut feeling as much as anything else. This poem feels done, or this poem feels that I can't do anything more with it.

KEVIN: And do you leave poems reluctantly?

RON: Good question. If it's worked really well, I'm happy to see it on the page and to reread it and think that's what I want it to do, there is that sense of pleasure. If I'm not sure that the poem is working, then I leave them with a sense of disappointment as much as anything else.

KEVIN: Is it more or less difficult to finish poems in more or less strict forms?

RON: I don't think it makes a difference. I've written a lot of sonnets . . . I don't often set out to write a sonnet, it simply falls into that form. At some stage of the writing process, I discover that there's a couple of lines that the poem really doesn't need and if I cut those out I've got a sonnet. I seem to write fourteen lines often, automatically.

But whether it's fourteen lines or forty lines, I get the feeling that this is the number of lines this poem needs, and it tells you when it's time to stop. Often it is a matter more of taking lines out than trying to push it into a particular shape or not. Whether it's a formal poem or a free verse poem, it knows when it's done.

KEVIN: And finally, is there anything your readers owe you?

RON: No. Your readers don't owe you anything. You owe the readers the opportunity to read a poem that will interest them, that will excite them. You hope that if they open one of your poems, if they start reading one of your poems, they will read it through to the end. But you can't expect it of them. They're doing you a favour because they're taking the trouble to read your poem.

NOTES

1   Deb Westbury was an Australian poet who died in 2018, as this book was being brought to completion

2   Hemingway, Ernest 1940 *For Whom the Bell Tolls*, New York: Charles Scribner

3   Forrest, Mabel 1909 'Boy-Dreams', in *Alpha Centauri*, Melbourne: Lothian

4   *Sotto* publishes news, views, interviews, poems and reviews of poets, poetry and poetic events across Australia. Source: AustLit (www.austlit.edu.au)

5   The South Coast Writers Centre are a not-for-profit organisation that provides professional development, information and networks for writers and readers on the South Coast and Southern Highland of NSW. Source: AustLit (www.austlit.edu.au)

6   Chloe Wilson is an editor and poet based in Melbourne

7   Youngstreet Poets, a Sydney group, is twenty or so members who meet monthly at New South Wales Writers' Centre and read one poem for group comment. Youngstreet Poets publish an anthology edited by a more established poet unconnected with the group. Source: AustLit (www.austlit.edu.au)

8   George Seferis (1900–1971) was a Greek poet, awarded the Nobel Prize in Literature in 1963

9   Brook Emery is a Sydney-based poet

10 Connie Barber (Constance Marjorie Barber) is an Australian painter and poet who died in 2014.

11 Alex Skovron is an editor and poet based in Melbourne

12 Rob Hood is an Australian story story writer

13 John Scott is an editor, translator and poet in Australia
14 Martin Duwell is a leading editor and reviewer of poetry in Australia
15 Geoff Page is a Canberra-based poet and reviewer of poetry
16 John Maxwell Coetzee is a South African-born writer, winner of the 2003 Nobel Prize in Literature, who became an Australian citizen in 2006

Poet biographical notes

Morose, counter-intuitive, something of a zany, **KEN BOLTON** cuts a moodily romantic figure within the dun Australian literary landscape, his name inevitably conjuring perhaps that best-known image of him, bow-tie askew, grinning cheerfully, at the wheel of his 1955 Jaguar D-type, *El Cid*. It is this image that also carries in its train the stories of later suffering—the affairs, the court appearances, the bad teeth—and, speaking of teeth, the beautiful poems wrenched from the teeth of despair & written on the wrist of happiness 'where happiness happens to like its poems written best' (in his inordinate phrase). Shearsman have published his *Selected Poems* &, more recently, *Species of Spaces*. Vagabond have just published *Starting at Basheer's*.

JUSTIN CLEMENS is the author of a number of books of poetry, including *Villain* (Hunter 2009) and *The Mundiad* (Hunter 2013). He is currently working on an Australian Research Council grant titled 'Australian Poetry Today,' and teaches at The University of Melbourne.

DIANE FAHEY is the author of thirteen poetry collections, most recently, *November Journal,* published by Whitmore Press in 2017. Diane received the ACT Government's Judith Wright Prize for *Sea Wall and River Light* in 2007. Other collections have been shortlisted for major poetry awards: *Metamorphoses, Mayflies in Amber, Listening to a Far Sea, The Wing Collection: New & Selected Poems* and *The Stone Garden: Poems from Clare*. Among her awards for individual poems are the John Shaw Neilson Poetry Prize, the Newcastle Poetry Prize and the Wesley Michel Wright Prize. Diane has been the recipient of a Felix Meyer Scholarship from the University of Melbourne, five literary grants from the Victorian and South Australian Governments, and six writer's grants from the Literature Board of the Australia Council of the Arts—the latest of which was to support the writing of a poetry collection set in the West of Ireland. She was chosen to take part in Australian Poetry's International Poetry Tour of Ireland in 2013.

Writing residencies she has been awarded have taken her to Venice, to the Tyrone Guthrie Centre, and Cill Rialaig Artists' Retreat, in Ireland, to Hawthornden Castle International Writers' Retreat in Scotland, and to Varuna, the National Writers House, and Bundanon Writers' and Artists' Retreat, both in N.S.W. Diane Fahey has been writer in residence at Ormond College at the University of Melbourne, and at the University of Adelaide. In 2000, she was awarded a PhD in Creative Writing from the University of Western Sydney for her study, 'Places and Spaces of the Writing Life'. Her website: dianefaheypoet.com

DR JENNIFER HARRISON is a Melbourne neuropsychiatrist and poet. She has published seven poetry collections and two anthologies of Australian poetry, including *Motherlode, Australian Women's Poetry 1986-2008* (Puncher & Wattmann 2009). Jennifer's collection *Colombine, New and Selected Poems* (Black Pepper 2010) was shortlisted for the Western Australian Premier's Prize. In 2011 Jennifer founded The Dax Poetry Collection at The Dax Centre, University of Melbourne, which houses the national collection of visual art created by people with lived experience of mental illness and psychological trauma. In 2012 she received the Christopher Brennan Award for sustained contribution to Australian poetry. Supported by a 2014 grant from the Literature Board of the Australia Council for the Arts, Jennifer's seventh poetry collection, *Anywhy*, was published in 2018 by Melbourne's Black Pepper.

JILL JONES has published eleven full-length books of poetry, including *Viva the Real* (UQP 2018), *Brink* (Five Islands Press 2017), *The Beautiful Anxiety* (Puncher & Wattmann 2014) which won the Victorian Premier's Prize for Poetry in 2015, and *Breaking the Days*, which won the Whitmore Press Manuscript Prize 2015 and was shortlisted for the 2017 NSW Premier's Literary Awards. Her work is represented in a number of major anthologies including the *Macquarie PEN Anthology of Australian Literature, Contemporary Australian Poetry* and *The Penguin Anthology of Australian Poetry*. With Scots-Australian poet Alison Flett, she publishes chapbooks through Little Windows

Press. In 2014 she was poet-in-residence at Stockholm University. She is a member of the J.M. Coetzee Centre for Creative Practice, University of Adelaide.

MIKE LADD was born to Australian parents in Berkeley, California in 1959, but grew up at Blackwood in the Adelaide hills. He has published nine books of poetry and prose, including the haibun *Karrawirra Parri: Walking the Torrens from Source to Sea*. His latest collection, *Invisible Mending*, was published by Wakefield Press in 2016. Mike was the founding producer and editor of *Poetica*, ABC Radio National's weekly poetry program, which ran from 1997 to 2015. Mike is based in Adelaide and is currently working on a radio ode to the Mallee. Earlier this year he was a guest of New Zealand's Writers and Readers Festival in Wellington.

RON PRETTY has been writing poetry for more than 40 years. His eighth book of poetry, *The Left Hand Mirror*, was published by Pitt Street Poetry in 2017. The third edition of his *Creating Poetry* was published by PSP in 2015 and reviewed in *Australian Book Review* in March 2016. He has taught writing in schools, universities and community groups throughout Australia and overseas. From 1983 to 1999 he was Head of Writing at the University of Wollongong, where he helped establish the South Coast Writers Centre. He published 230 books by Australian poets in the twenty years 1987–2007, as publisher for Five Islands Press. Between 2000 and 2007, he ran the Poetry Australia Foundation. He taught creative writing at the University of Melbourne 2001–2007. He was editor of the literary/arts magazine *scarp*, published by the University of Wollongong, from 1984 to 1999. He was managing editor of *Blue Dog: Australian Poetry* 2002–2007.

ROBYN ROWLAND is an Irish-Australian citizen living in both countries. She regularly works in Turkey. She has written thirteen books, ten of poetry. Her latest books are *Mosaics from the Map* (Doire Press, Galway, 2018) and her bi-lingual *This Intimate War Gallipoli/ Çanakkale 1915—İçli Dışlı Bir Savaş: Gelibolu/Çanakkale 1915* (Five

Islands, 2015; repub., Spinifex Press, Australia, 2018; Turkish translations, Mehmet Ali Çelikel). Robyn's poetry appears in national and international journals and in over forty anthologies, including eight editions of *Best Australian Poems*. She has read and taught in Ireland for 35 years and has been invited to read in India, Portugal, Ireland, the UK, the USA, Greece, Austria, Bosnia, Serbia, Turkey and Italy, where, along with Canada, Spain and Japan, she has also been published, sometimes in translation. She has two CDs of poetry, *Off the Tongue* and *Silver Leaving—Poems & Harp* with Lynn Saoirse. She has been filmed reading for the *National Irish Poetry Reading Archive*, James Joyce Library, University College Dublin, available on YouTube. Robyn has received grants from the Literature Board of the Australian Council and the CAL Cultural Fund. She was a Board member, Poetry Australia Foundation, 2004–2006; Deputy Chair, Board Australian Poetry Centre, 2007–2009; Member, Australia Poetry Ltd, National Advisory Council 2010–2013. See www.robynrowland.com

Originally from Western Australia, **PHILIP SALOM** now lives in North Melbourne. He has published three novels and fourteen books of poetry. In 2017 *Waiting*, his most recent novel, was shortlisted for the Miles Franklin Award, the Prime Minister's Award and the Victorian Premiers Prize. Better known as a poet of diversity and challenge, Philip Salom's other awards include twice winning the Commonwealth Poetry Book Prize in London, the Western Australia Premiers Prize (three times) and two wins in the prestigious Newcastle Poetry Prize. In 2003 he was recognised with the Christopher Brennan Award, which is Australia's prestigious lifetime award for poets, acknowledging 'poetry of sustained quality and distinction'. His most recent poetry collection is the trilogy *Alterworld* (Puncher and Wattmann, 2015), and a new novel *The Returns* is forthcoming from Transit Lounge in 2019.

MICHAEL SHARKEY has written reviews, essays and poems since the late 1960s, during engagement with universities in New Zealand, Australia, China and Germany, where he variously taught literature in

English, Australian studies, rhetorical analysis, and formal writing. His background also includes publishing, literary promotion, and conducting writing workshops. He has edited poetry magazines, most recently the *Australian Poetry Journal* from 2014 through to 2016. He is the author of biographical essays in the *Australian Dictionary of Biography*, the *Dictionary of New Zealand Biography* and other publications, and his biography of the NZ-Australian poet David McKee Wright, *Apollo in George Street*, was published by Puncher & Wattmann in 2012. He has edited a collection of Australian humour, and written critical essays on individual poets' and novelists' productions. A collection of such prose, *The Poetic Eye: Occasional Writings 1982–2012,* edited by Gordon Collier, was published by Brill Rodopi in 2016. As poet, Michael Sharkey is author of a dozen collections, the latest of which are *Another Fine Morning in Paradise* (2012) and *The Real World (and Other Poems),* 2017. His anthology of 25 Victorian Australian Women poets of World War One, titled *Many Such as She*, was published by Walleah Press in 2018.

Editor biographical notes

KEVIN BROPHY's latest book is *Look at the Lake* (Puncher & Wattmann), a record of two years spent in the Aboriginal Community of Mulan in the Great Sandy Desert. A Professor emeritus at the University of Melbourne, he is a poet-in-residence at the Keesing Studio in Paris, 2019–20.

MONICA CARROLL is a researcher and writer in Canberra. She has published papers on phenomenology, poetry and philosophy. Her writing and research blog can be found at monica-carroll.com.

JEN WEBB is Director of the Centre for Creative and Cultural Research at the University of Canberra, and co-editor of the scholarly journal *Axon: Creative Explorations* and the literary journal *Meniscus*. Her latest poetry collection is *Moving Targets* (Recent Work Press, 2018). She was lead investigator on the Australian Research Council project DP130100402, which generated these interviews.